SUPERIOR

Journeys On An Inland Sea

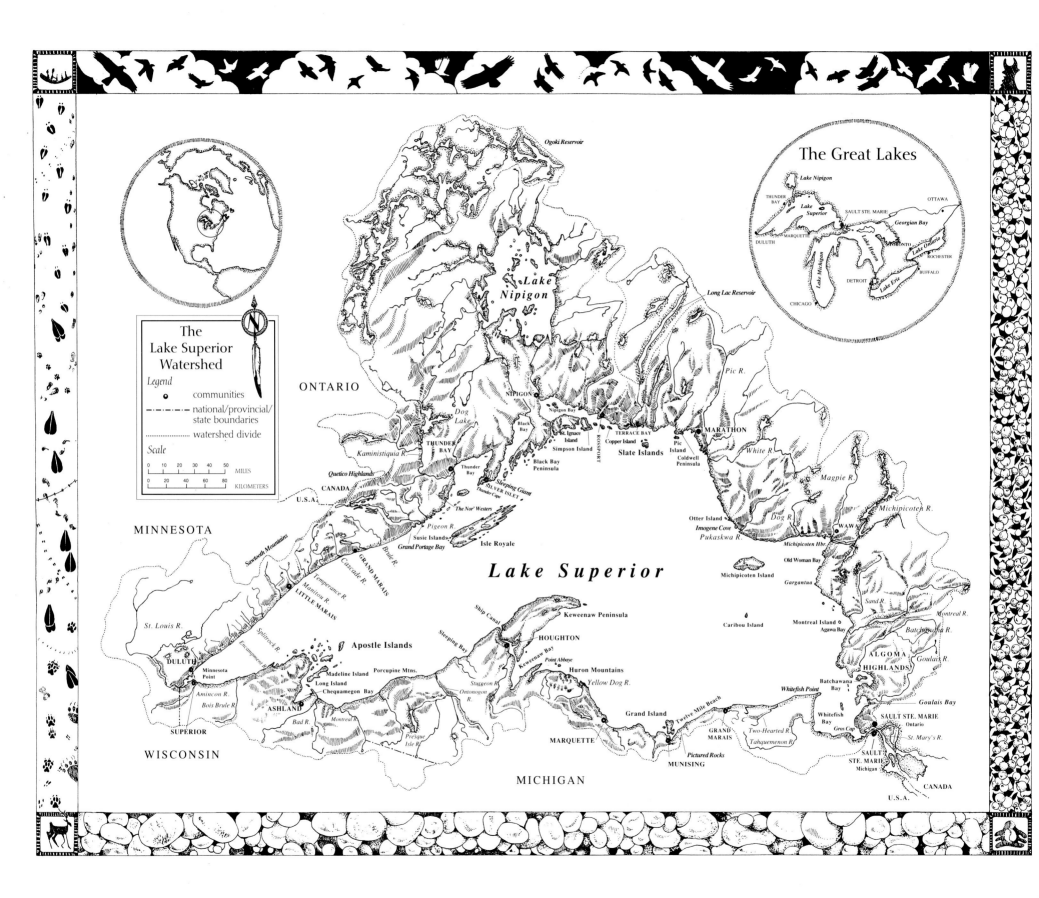

The Great Lakes

Lake Nipigon
THUNDER BAY
Lake Superior
SAULT STE. MARIE
OTTAWA
DULUTH
MARQUETTE
Georgian Bay
Lake Huron
TORONTO
Lake Ontario
ROCHESTER
Lake Michigan
DETROIT
Lake Erie
BUFFALO
CHICAGO

The Lake Superior Watershed

Legend

- communities
- ·–·–· national/provincial/ state boundaries
- ········· watershed divide

Scale

```
0   10  20  30  40  50   MILES
0    20    40    60    80  KILOMETERS
```

ONTARIO

Ogoki Reservoir

Lake Nipigon

Long Lac Reservoir

Pic R.

NIPIGON

Nipigon Bay

MARATHON

Dog Lake

Black Bay

St. Ignace Island

TERRACE BAY

ROSSPORT

Pic Island

Coldwell Peninsula

White R.

THUNDER BAY

Kaministiquia R.

Copper Island

Simpson Island

Slate Islands

Magpie R.

Quetico Highlands

Thunder Bay

Black Bay Peninsula

CANADA

U.S.A.

Sleeping Giant
SILVER ISLET
Thunder Cape

The Nor' Westers

Michipicoten R.

Otter Island

Dog R.

WAWA

MINNESOTA

Pigeon R.

Susie Islands

Isle Royale

Imogene Cove
Pukaskwa R.

Michipicoten Hbr.

Old Woman Bay

Sawtooth Mountains

GRAND MARAIS

Cascade R.

Brule R.

Temperance R.

Grand Portage Bay

Lake Superior

Gargantua

Sand R.

St. Louis R.

Manitou R.

LITTLE MARAIS

Michipicoten Island

Caribou Island

Montreal Island

Agawa Bay

Batchawana R.

Splitrock R.

Encampment R.

Apostle Islands

Ship Canal

Keweenaw Peninsula

ALGOMA HIGHLANDS

Goulais R.

DULUTH

Minnesota Point

Madeline Island

Long Island

Chequamegon Bay

Porcupine Mtns.

Sleeping Bay

HOUGHTON

Keweenaw Bay

Point Abbaye

Huron Mountains

Yellow Dog R.

Batchawana Bay

Whitefish Point

Goulais Bay

Amnicon R.

Bois Brule R.

ASHLAND

Bad R.

Montreal R.

Ontonagon R.

Sturgeon R.

Grand Island

Twelve Mile Beach

GRAND MARAIS

Two-Hearted R.

Tahquemenon R.

Whitefish Bay

Gros Cap

SAULT STE. MARIE
Ontario

St. Mary's R.

SUPERIOR

Presque Isle R.

MARQUETTE

Pictured Rocks

MUNISING

SAULT STE. MARIE
Michigan

WISCONSIN

MICHIGAN

CANADA

U.S.A.

SUPERIOR

Journeys On An Inland Sea

GARY & JOANIE McGUFFIN

Stoddart · A BOSTON MILLS PRESS BOOK

CANADIAN CATALOGUING IN PUBLICATION DATA

McGuffin, Gary
Superior : journeys on an inland sea

ISBN 1-55046-067-6

1. Canoes and canoeing – Superior, Lake.
2. Superior, Lake – Description and travel.
I. McGuffin, Joanie. II. Title

GV776.15.S86M24 1995   917.13'12   C95-930792-3

First published in 1995 by
The Boston Mills Press
132 Main Street
Erin, Ontario
N0B 1T0
1-800-565-3111

Second printing, April 1996

An affiliate of
Stoddart Publishing Co. Limited
34 Lesmill Road
North York, Ontario, Canada
M3B 2T6

Design by Gillian Stead
Map and illustrations by Joanie McGuffin
Printed in Canada by Friesen Printers

OVERLEAF: *Greeted by the swirl of ring-billed gulls at Caribou Island in Thunder Bay.*

The publisher gratefully acknowledges the support of the Canada Council and Ontario Arts Council
in the development of writing and publishing in Canada.

This book has been printed using vegetable-based inks on high-quality paper that has been manufactured without polluting our waterways with toxic substances such as dioxins. Phoeno-Grand 100 lb. text is a premium coated paper made with totally chlorine-free pulp.

This paper is available from
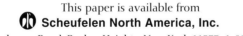 Scheufelen North America, Inc.
99 Powerhouse Road, Roslyn Heights, New York 11577 1-800-551-2470

SCHEUFELEN NORTH AMERICA, INC. is honored to have been able to play a role in the preparation of this fine environmental publication.
Using 100% chlorine-free pulp, we manufacture premium, age-resistant, quality papers which are non-toxic and meet ISO 9001 certification standards.
At Scheufelen, we feel that environmental protection starts with the selection of environmentally compatible raw materials and continues on through
the manufacturing process, including the proper re-use and safe disposal of waste materials. This should be a universal goal for all industries, especially
those who have been blessed enough to grow and prosper from our natural resources. We can show our appreciation for our prosperity by leaving a clean,
safe environment of which our children can be proud, thus encouraging them to contribute in kind to each subsequent generation.

For all those whose songs fill the sky, earth and water,
reminding us of the myriad of life-forms that make our human lives
not only far more mysterious, but possible.

Wolves at play

CONTENTS

A moon rising over the Susie Islands illuminates our idyllic campsite on a cobble beach. Writing in the journal to record the day's experiences and marking the maps while pondering the unknown course lying ahead, was part of our evening ritual around the campfire.

INTRODUCTION

JOURNEYS GERMINATE LIKE SEEDS. THEY DEPEND UPON THE FERTILITY OF THE MIND THEY FALL UPON. They may originate inside and outside ourselves — from stories we have been told, dreams that inspire us, people we meet, or wild places that touch us. Gary and I have found that once one of these magic seeds has taken root, our minds nurture it until the urge to undertake the journey will not go away. The desire builds slowly at first but picks up momentum once we make a commitment to each other and begin planning.

For both of us, this way of life began with parents whose love for one another was, and still is, rooted in their shared experiences in the outdoors. Their respect and appreciation for the processes and creatures of the natural world greatly influenced our young and inquisitive minds. We both grew up in Ontario, Gary in London and I in Thornhill. Although our homes were in cities, we each lived near a forest divided by a river valley. Gary's forest had huge buttonwood and beech trees, salmon spawning in the creeks, pheasants, mink, fox and white-tailed deer. My forest was a mixture of pine, sugar maple, willows and old apple trees. There were ducks, woodpeckers, thrushes, warblers, rabbits, raccoons, squirrels, and even the occasional peregrine falcon, red-tailed hawk and snowy owl. These were special, wild places that our parents encouraged us to explore during all seasons of the year.

Lake Superior is a celebration of clean, fresh water; the simple, magical fluid flowing through every living thing.

Every summer we migrated north to cottages our parents had built: Gary to Temagami and I to Muskoka. It was in these two places that the journey seeds began to flourish. We swam in water so pure we could drink it. We learned to paddle canoes and, by doing so, gained the freedom to explore the shorelines where the loons nested and the beavers built their lodges.

The similarities in our childhood experiences extended through the seasons. With our parents, we hiked in autumn woodlands, catching colored leaves and listening for the geese flying south. We greeted winter with equal enthusiasm, donning snowshoes, skis or skates to follow animal tracks in the woods and explore frozen ponds. The journeys that we have undertaken together as adults began, for both of us, in childhood, when we learned the physical skills necessary for outdoor adventuring, along with an appreciation for life and a basic understanding of survival in all seasons.

The desire to know Lake Superior developed a life of its own through the stories our parents told. The wild places they described often seemed to us to be more exotic and exciting than those in fairy tales. The eastern and northern shores of Lake Superior were among those places. The very word *Superior* conjured a grand image in our young minds — not to mention the wonderful images evoked by such names as Pancake Bay, Old Woman Bay, the Sleeping Giant, and by the ancient pictographs of indigenous people. There were stories describing the great sweeps of sand beach, enormous black cliffs, foaming whitewater rivers jumping with salmon and trout, and hikes at the edge of a lake so huge it was blue for as far as the eye could see. Finally, in 1983, while on our way to the Beaufort Sea by canoe, we met Lake Superior for the first time. Three years later, we arrived on her shores again, this time on bicycles bound for the Atlantic coast. Our memories and journal entries from those two trips show where the journeys converged on Superior's shores and where a promise was made.

July 10, 1983

Gary and I were partway across Canada on a two-season 6,000-mile (10,000 km) canoe voyage from the Gulf of St. Lawrence to Tuktoyaktuk on the Beaufort Sea. What lay before us in the next three to four weeks could well be the most challenging section of the entire trip. Neither the Atlantic nor the Arctic coasts, nor the broadest and swiftest of rivers could stir the kind of trepidation we felt about navigating the 500-mile (800 km) north shore of Lake Superior. The picture in our minds was colored by our readings from early travelers and traders and, of course, the stories our parents told. It was a place of supreme beauty and notorious storms, a place of rocky, lonely, wild shores, and a place in which the record of the Earth's evolution was laid bare by the glaciers 10,000 years ago.

A late autumn storm on Mica Bay sends waves crashing through black shoals and against sheer cliffs in an awesome display of power.

We paddled the last few miles up the St. Mary's River from Lake Huron and entered the locks at Sault Ste. Marie. As the water filled the canal, our canoe rose to meet the largest expanse of fresh water on earth. Lake Superior taught us to respect her on our first day out when high waves and strong winds caught us midway on a crossing of Goulais Bay. After that first fearful experience, we vowed to make best use of every moment of calm weather. Unbeknownst to us, a stable weather system was settling in for the rest of July. Before sunup, we were on the water. Day in and day out, we were covering between 50 and 60 miles (80 and 100 km) before nightfall.

The experience of canoeing on Lake Superior blurred into one big impression. Brilliant sunsets flooded the evening skies, distant islands melted into faraway horizons, and glimpses of black bears, timber wolves, moose, otters and eagles left us with a deep impression of a powerful, wild and pristine place. Two weeks later we reached Grand Portage and traveled west away from Lake Superior, still more than a year from our Arctic destination.

Overlooking Paradise Island's reefs, red rock and raised beaches. Behind it lies Owl Island. The tiny strip of water visible between St. Ignace Island and the distant horizon is the Nipigon Channel, where we camped the first night of our journey.

June 19, 1986

Outside the RCMP depot in Dawson City, Yukon, we sifted through our mail. There was our first prepackaged box with film and dried food supplies that would see us through to Whitehorse, letters from our families and friends, some additional foul-weather clothing, and a postcard from Lillian Wolter.

> Dear CBC Morningside,
>
> I have been following your interviews with the young couple journeying from Tuktoyaktuk, N.W.T., to Newfoundland on their bicycles. I would like very much for them to visit me at Kama Bay where they can experience a real Finnish sauna and an invigorating swim in Superior, the world's largest lake! I don't know when and if they will pass my way but could you be so kind as to pass along my card to Gary and Joanie. I wish them all the best of luck.

We sent a reply thanking her for the invitation. With months and thousands of miles ahead of us, we had no idea if and when we would meet one another.

By late August, the West Coast mountains, the Queen Charlotte Islands and the Prairies were behind us. The roller-coaster road traversing Superior's north shore lay ahead. Pedaling east out of Thunder Bay, we rode far above the lake on pavement laid over an ancient beachline that existed at the end of the last ice age. All day we thought of the people who had lived here long ago, traveling and hunting in the north shore canyons. And we thought of the people living here now. We arrived on Kama Bay at day's end. An unforgettable landscape greeted us. Localized rain and snow squalls sweeping across the bay were colored bronze by the setting sun. Steep-walled mesas of shale rising to the north and east shone blood-red and purple. A well-rehearsed movie scene could not have been staged more perfectly, for the woman waving excitedly to us from the highway overlook turned out to be Lillian Wolter. She treated us to supper, a sauna and a swim in the moonlight. With our eyes, we followed the silver path shimmering across the bay. It led to the dark shapes of far-off islands. A longing to exchange bicycles for canoes tugged at us both that night as we listened to the soft lapping of water against sand. The following morning after breakfast, Lillian accompanied us to another lookout further along the road where we had a grand view of Nipigon Bay and St. Ignace Island. As we prepared to depart, Gary hugged Lillian and assured her that we would return. "One day, Joanie and I are going to paddle all the way around Lake Superior and we will begin right here from your cottage on Kama Bay."

She beamed with pleasure. "Have a safe journey, kids! Write me when you get home." A promise to ourselves was sealed. We would canoe around Lake Superior.

A mackerel sky reflected in the calm waters of Thunder Bay foretells of approaching winds and changing weather.
In the first days of our trip, the vast water-space lying always to our left felt both formidable and awe-inspiring.

THE JOURNEY SOUTH

Kama Bay to the St. Louis River

June

THE JOURNEY WAS AS NATURAL AS FOLLOWING A CIRCLE. THE BEGINNING AND COMPLETION OF THE ROUTE
around Lake Superior would be in Kama Bay, the northernmost point on the lake. We decided to canoe
in a counterclockwise direction, flowing with the lake's currents like Paddle-to-the-Sea, a carved
wooden character in a childhood story by Holling C. Holling.

Superior is the most expansive lake on earth. Its area of 32,000 square miles (82,000 km²) would
cover the province of New Brunswick with room to spare, or the states of Vermont, New Hampshire,
Connecticut and Massachusetts combined. A rock dropped into the water over the lake's deepest spot

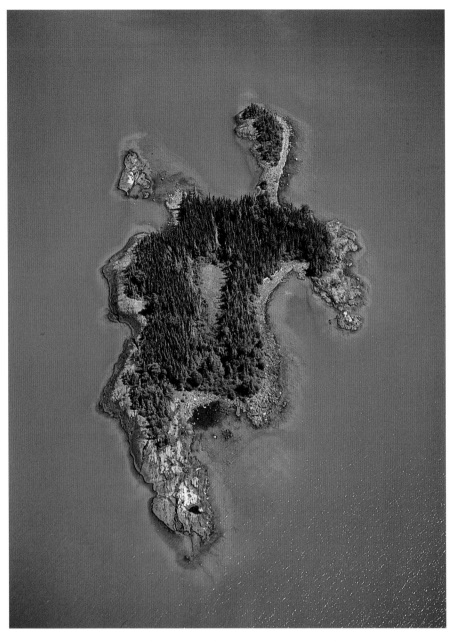

Quigley Island in Moffat Strait is, to us, the Dancing Woman. Winds stir the suspended sediments in the vast shallows of the Nipigon Bay area, turning the waters a pale, opaque green.

would sink 1,330 feet (450 m) before coming to rest on the bottom. Superior's enormous size can also be described by its volume of water: 3,000 cubic miles (6,500 km³), enough to cover the North and South American continents a foot deep. A drop of water entering Superior from rain clouds or rivers can circulate the basin for two hundred years before it flows down the St. Mary's River at Sault Ste. Marie. More than two hundred rivers flow in, but the St. Mary's is the only one flowing out.

Even the distance around the shoreline is impressive. On our map, Gary laid a string around the lake, weaving it in and out of all the bays. To this length, he added the measured distance around the islands and came up with almost 3,000 miles (4,800 km). Each morning, it takes the sun a full half hour to illuminate the lake on its longest east-to-west crossing from Batchawana Bay to the St. Louis River. The latitude difference between the most northerly point at Kama Bay and the most southerly at Munising is evident in the forest change from jack pine and balsam fir to white pine and sugar maples. Superior's grand size, combined with its location at the crossroads of air currents from all corners of the continent, grants the lake a sense of independence. It creates its own weather patterns, establishing rules about the ebb and flow of seasonal life. The sheer size deters crossings by hawks, eagles, ospreys and falcons, who prefer to fly the eastern and western shores during spring and fall migrations.

The morning we set off on our journey dawned clear and calm at Kama Point. The silent expectancy hanging over those green waters was almost palpable. I was sure our two shiny red canoes could feel the lake's tiny waves tickling their hulls, coaxing them to float free from the sand beach.

Our previous experiences traveling long distances in canoes and kayaks helped us choose our craft for this voyage. We felt it would be safer to go solo as well as more companionable in the long run. We could paddle side by side and carry on a conversation, which can be difficult in a long, tandem canoe. We could also paddle at our individual speeds, choosing our respective distance from shore depending on what we wanted to see. (Our journey across Canada taught us that we need to balance the time we spend together with time alone.) Just having another canoe to look at was encouraging on an open stretch of water. These solo craft had unique characteristics that combined features from both canoes and sea kayaks. We sat in the canoes with our legs outstretched. Our feet rested on adjustable braces, which were attached to the rudder by two cables, enabling us to steer the canoes with our feet. Our contoured seats, comfortably padded, could adjust to three positions, the highest position for comfort and the lowest one for stability in rough water. The seats could also be flipped

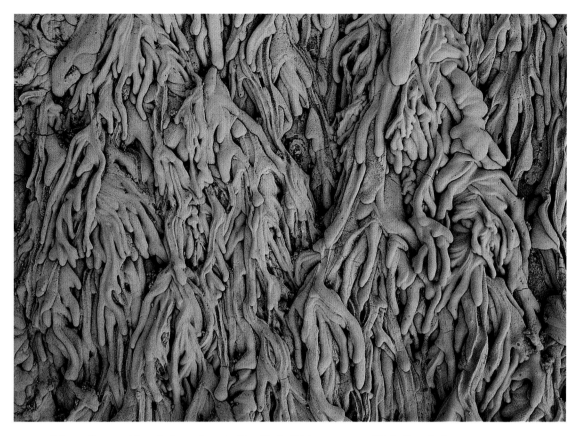

Talcum-fine sand found along the east side of Lake Nipigon, source of Lake Superior's largest tributary, thaws and freezes between sun and shade, forming kelplike formations.

over to form carrying yokes for portaging. The canoes were partially decked and, with the addition of a sprayskirt that covered the open cockpit, we would stay warm and dry in all kinds of weather.

Large packs containing clothing and camping gear had been stowed behind the seats while food packs shoved toward the bow of each canoe balanced the weight nicely. Our camera boxes lay on the floor in front of our seats, and small bags containing binoculars, sunscreen, sunglasses, notebooks and snacks hung from hooks below the front coaming on the canoe decks. In this way, the bags and cameras were handy during the day.

It was early and we were eager to be underway, so we pushed our canoes off the beach and stepped in. We engaged our rudders, placed our feet on the braces, then raised our paddles to wave good-bye to Lillian and the friends on shore who had come to see us off.

One of the finest examples of the six-sided, honeycombed columnar basalt on Lake Superior can be seen on the southwestern side of Simpson Island.

For half a day we just enjoyed the feeling of beginning another journey. At the mouth of the Nipigon River, we glided in below the white cliffs half hidden by patches of lichens, mosses and the tangle of gnarly old cedar roots. It was here, at the mouth of Superior's largest tributary, at a time when the world was a quieter place, that the Anishnabe told stories of hearing the soft laughter of the Maymaygwaysiwuk. These little people with their round faces and flat noses were believed to bestow misfortune on those who tried to hurt or hinder them. We had heard of their homes in underwater caves beneath these cliffs and of the legendary subterranean passages that led to the offering rocks on Lake Nipigon. We searched eagerly for symbols painted long ago by Anishnabe artists on the face of this cliff. A disturbance on the water surface caught our attention. It was a frog floating nearly lifeless, paralyzed with cold. Gary quickly scooped it up. Paddling over to a sun–warmed ledge, he left it to recuperate. To the people who once lived here, the frog was the singer of the song that calls the rain to Earth, and the harbinger of all initiations by water. At that moment we both glanced up to discover a red ochre painting of a froglike figure leaping across the rock. I copied a likeness of the painting on the first page of my logbook, a symbolic beginning to our own initiation by water, a long journey by canoe around the lake. When we went back to check on the condition of the frog, it was gone. Gary thought the ledge seemed a fitting place to leave a small pouch of tobacco.

That evening, we chose a sand spit in the Nipigon Strait for our camp. Falling into the comfortable, simple routine of traveling together, we unloaded the canoes and pulled the home–sewn tarpaulins over the open cockpits to keep the contents dry. The evening sky darkened without stars, covered by a soft gray blanket of cloud. We were expecting rain by morning. Minutes later we had completed the task of setting up the tent, with everything neatly arranged inside.

Broken up by islands, coves, harbors, caves and cliffs, St. Ignace Island's south shore is like a ragged tear compared to the straight high bluffs of its northern side. We have spent days exploring this area in canoes, kayaks and on foot.

Among the pleasures of journeying are the rituals of establishing a new camp,
savoring a different view from the tent door each morning, and packing up to move on.

Gary pulled up a log for a seat and made a small fire while I went down to the shore to fill our water container. As I crouched there, looking back up the channel from where we had come that day, I noticed a strange sight. Carving thin, arrow-straight lines across the smooth surface were the dorsal fins of some large fish. I called Gary down and together we watched them swim toward us and pass close by. Although neither of us had ever seen coasters, we had heard of this unique species of speckled trout that cruise the open lake, only returning to rivers to spawn. Once plentiful, they are now something of a rarity. They were heading in the direction we would be going tomorrow, out past the protected channel where the horizon met the silver sea.

Later on, by firelight, Gary perused the maps while I scribbled a couple of pages in the new journal. Logbooks kept on journeys are a treasure, for they help restore the moments, the events and feelings that later become hazy

Interpreting a journey through painting, photography and writing is a way to preserve and share one's personal story of the land. The colors and textures, weather and landforms on Lake Superior were unlike anything we had experienced before.

through time. The real character of those cherished memories is not so much what is visible to the eye, but the feelings evoked by the senses of smell, taste, touch and sound. This place looks like an ordinary sand point jutting into the Nipigon Strait, but it soon becomes home. It is the place where we first camped on our journey around the lake. This day may have seemed ordinary and uneventful, but it will always hold special significance. It was the first day of our voyage.

Perhaps because we enjoy keeping our own logbook, we find historical journals particularly entertaining. I had packed copies of several old maps and diaries from early travelers describing the places that we would be passing through. These people lived in tents and traveled in canoes, so we shared similar experiences despite the span of time separating us. Their writing gave us a measure of change. We would come to know how much had been altered and how much was as they had seen it. That night I burned half a candle reading from E. E. Millard's 1917 journal, *Days on the Nepigon*.

The stretch of river between Virgin Falls and Miners' Rapids to Canal Rapids, like many another length of the stream, is charmingly vagrant. More than that and perhaps worse, it is delightfully tipsy. It hurries and loiters, dawdles and whirls; it is quiet and boisterous, and with many a merry ripple rushes into whirlpools of disorder, and out into the sunshine, then staggers back into the shadows of great rocks and tall trees, babbling in a maelstrom of unrest, "springing over obstacles, frequently going astray, but always coming out right further along, in spite of everything"; and while perplexing cross-currents, backsets and rapids impede its progress, it manages, like a thing of life, to stutter th-th-the river is fu-fu-full of trout; they only need ca-ca-catching. Surely it classes with the notable trout streams of the world. It is radiant with promises, its whole length a cheerful ripple of invitation; and we are promptly busy with the important object of our outing, one rod at the foot of the falls, the other from the rocks near camp, an advantageous and unobstructed point for the fly thrower.

Three days into our travels, we reached the islands located off the south side of the Black Bay Peninsula. Still feeling exposed and vulnerable to the vast open horizon, we slipped across the wide opening of Shesheeb Bay and sought shelter in the channels between Brodeur, Lasher, Borden, Swede and dozens of smaller islands. Their close presence comforted us. The thick green walls of cedar and the black cliffs encrusted with rock tripe and orange lichens made for some enjoyable paddling. Gary frequently compared this type of environment with places remembered from his childhood, canoeing on the more sheltered, smaller water bodies in Temagami. However, we discovered the land was not nearly so friendly and inviting when we wanted to come ashore. The forest bristled out, prickly and unwelcoming.

By afternoon the outer islands were behind us. To the north, puffy white cumulus clouds were mushrooming into anvil-shaped thunderheads. Between them and us, a heavy rain swept across the hills, snuffing out the land but not the sound of the electrical storm riding the fast-approaching cold front. A sudden stiff wind wrinkled the water's surface. The first small waves were caught by the wind like sails. They grew quickly, sinking deeper and rising higher until the white edges were being torn away to mix with the rain.

Long tentacles of fog came probing in from the opposite direction, smothering the comforting landmark of two broad, round hills identified as The Paps on our map. The fog was advancing as fast as the storm, dissolving rock, water and sky in its wake. Our fear riveted our attention to the task at hand.

The boreal forest hugging the shoreline from Michipicoten Harbour to Thunder Bay extends north to the treeless tundra. Tamarack, birch, balsam, jack pine, black spruce, labrador tea, reindeer lichen, blueberries and sphagnum moss are among the variety of species that make up the largest and one of the most important forest types on earth.

Skiing to the brink of Ouimet Canyon's western rim is a knee-shaking experience.
Columns of rock continue to break off, widening the half-mile-long chasm.

I was using my whole body to plant the paddle and propel myself forward toward the nearest island. Just then I lost sight of Gary as everything vanished in fog, rain and wind. I was alone on the battleground of the thunderbirds and the sea gods. I quelled the rising panic by paddling harder. Then I heard Gary's shout of encouragement, "Follow me." I was so near shore when the faint outline of the island appeared that it startled me. I hurried on, since I could now see the red shape of Gary's canoe just ahead.

We entered the calm waters immensely relieved. The familiar steep black rock formed a wall to one side of the bay, but as we followed it back, the bottom came up to meet the low shoreline in a thin rim of sand. Now feeling extremely thankful, we landed, unloaded the canoes and searched for a place to put up the tent. Pushing back scraggly branches that fringed the forest edge, we clambered over the deadfall and drift and disappeared into the shadow of the dark forest. In a place scented with black spruce, balsam and cedar, we pitched our tent on a soft bed of trailing ground pine. We nestled into our dry, warm shelter, cooking a simple dinner in the tent's vestibule.

All night, the damp, cold fingers of fog groped blindly through the trees. The battle raged on, wind and rain roaring through the forest canopy, snapping limbs from groaning trees. Snuggling deeper into our sleeping bags, we floated in and out of consciousness until, near dawn, we were aware that the battle cry had died away. Scrambling out of the tent, we were greeted by fresh, sweet, rain–washed smells of earth and air. The greens so lush, the blues so vivid. The lake was breathing quietly, filling in our footprints as we walked the narrow beach. A pair of mergansers were threading their way around the shore, darting and diving for minnows. The morning was alive with twittering chickadees and kinglets, and the spring song of robins.

During the early summer, when the air passing over the lake is still so much warmer than the water, fog is never far away. It is a strange creature. Sometimes it puffs aimlessly along, but at other times, it moves more stealthily, creeping, probing, scouting, searching out the unwary. If it moved in really thick while we were on the water, Gary and I would appear to one another as merely dark shadows. The unseeable shore was identified by the sound of water meeting rock or sand. If we paddled by a cliff, the feel of choppy, rebounding waves told us so. The fresh, rich earthy scents of the forest carried on the fog told us much about the shoreline even if we couldn't see it. Muffled quacking followed by slapping water and purring wingbeats was the sound of a merganser pair sizing us up, dropping into the water, then taking flight. My favorite fogs were those that acted like theatrical curtains, hiding one scene, unveiling another. At one point, the fog lifted its cloak to reveal the boiler from a shipwreck resting on a shoal. Beyond it, a lifeboat tucked into the shoreline undergrowth came

A dead spruce covered in old-man's beard lichen grows through the weathered hull of a wrecked lifeboat. Nearby lies a ship's boiler. Such discoveries conjured visions of black nights and dark, rolling seas.

into view. A spruce tree was growing up through its pierced hull. I tried to imagine the disaster that brought it to this final resting place. A dark night with an east wind roaring across the raging sea. Freezing waters rolling over a foundering ship. A terrified crew scrambling aboard the small lifeboats rising and falling in the monstrous waves. Someone manning the oars while others bail frantically.

On the afternoon following the big storm, as we crossed the mouth of Black Bay, a mysterious current swept us through the gap between Edward and Ariel Islands. Eddy pools had formed on either side of this river-within-a-lake. We were so intrigued that we turned around to paddle back again, but when we did, we found the current had switched direction and was now rushing back the other way. We later discovered that these small tidelike movements, called seiches, are not created by the gravitational pull of the moon (as ocean tides are) but rather result from variations in barometric pressure over the surface of such a huge lake. Seiches, which act rather like water sloshing back and forth in a bathtub, were particularly noticeable in the narrow openings to shallow bays. Sometimes when we camped on a sand beach, Gary would place an upright stick near the water's edge, and we could watch the lake breathing, inhaling and exhaling, mostly by inches, but sometimes the rise would be more than a foot.

The wind also has a strong effect upon the lake level. Onshore winds can cause the waves to reach great heights, climbing the cliffs and spraying the forest. Strong offshore winds have the opposite effect, creating wide beaches where there were none the night before.

Near the Black Bay Peninsula, we tow our Crazy Carpet sleds past meltwaters. Winter camping and ski touring is most enjoyable in March, when the days are longer and warmer and the firm snow crust makes for ideal traveling conditions.

During an early winter ski camping trip in Sleeping Giant Provincial Park, Gary photographed Thunder Cape,
which forms the tip of the Giant's feet.

Within less than a week, we had arrived at the Sleeping Giant, the huge landform that dominates the scene in the northwestern corner of Lake Superior. The peninsula's profile resembles a giant lying down with his chest to the sky. The soles of his feet form the steepest vertical cliffs in Ontario, more than 850 feet (300 m) high. Several traditional stories explain its origins, but I most like the one about the silver of Silver Islet, the place where we would be camping that night.

One day, long ago, Nanabijou, son of the west wind, and a great teacher and protector of the Anishnabe, was scratching at a rock when suddenly it glimmered with silver. He feared Anishnabe land could be taken away if anyone were to discover it. At the time he had been told by the Great Spirit that strange fair-skinned people were coming from afar and that he was to greet them in friendship. To protect the people, Nanabijou gathered everyone together. They dug up all the silver and then buried it again under a little island just offshore. All were made to swear they would never tell anyone. However, one greedy man could not resist keeping some of the silver to construct weapons for himself. But when he died in battle, the silver came into the hands of his enemies, who believed it could be traded with the white man. A thunderbird told Nanabijou that the white traders were being led back to find the silver. In his fury, Nanabijou forgot his duty of greeting the newcomers with friendliness. He raised a storm to sink their approaching party of canoes. The act made the Great Spirit very unhappy. As a punishment, Nanabijou was turned to stone. He fell backward into the lake and became the Sleeping Giant.

We paddled over to the small island where Nanabijou and his people had buried the silver. It was less than a mile offshore from the summer community of Silver Islet. Peering down into the clear waters beneath our canoes, we saw remnants of the cribbings that had once supported the structure of a mine. More than 120 years ago, on a July

Rising from the foot of the Sleeping Giant are some of the highest vertical cliffs in Ontario. Canoeing beneath them, we were fortunate to see peregrine falcons, the magnificent avian predators that nest here.

The profile of the Sleeping Giant was a constant landmark for us for three days of paddling.

---

day much like this one, surveyors from the Montreal Mining Company decided to use Skull Rock as a transit base. The fluke discovery of native silver caused a flurry of activity as the surveyors grabbed any kind of tool they could find to pry off pieces of the precious metal.

Within two years, the Silver Islet Consolidated Mining and Land Company had started up a mining operation. The local Anishnabe warned there would be serious consequences for those who aroused Nanabijou's anger by burrowing into the earth for that silver. But they were ignored. White miners and their families moved in for the next fifteen years.

The mine, which eventually produced three and a half million dollars in silver, was the most lucrative of its kind in the mid-nineteenth century. But, ironically, an equivalent amount of money was required just to keep the mine running. To accommodate all the mining equipment, huge cribbings of white pine timbers were constructed to enlarge Silver Island four times its original size. But Superior's autumn storms mocked the enterprise by continually dismantling the elaborate structure, hurling the enormous timbers against shore as if they were toothpicks.

Over the years, a high human price was also paid by the miners who descended those 1200-foot (365 m) shafts far below Lake Superior. Steam-powered pumps had been responsible for keeping the mine from flooding. It may have been the shipment of coal that arrived too late one fall, or that the mining company coffers ran dry, but the pumps stopped running and Silver Islet Mine flooded and closed forever. Many of the miners packed up and left, towing their homes across the ice to present-day Thunder Bay. The buildings that remained at the town site have since been painted and restored as summer cottages.

From our vantage point offshore, we could see the entire community. The large, brown, two-and-a-half-story general store just up from the public dock was a familiar sight from several years back when we first canoed by. Back then, the old store had been boarded up. We were surprised and delighted this time to walk through open doors. The polished pine board floor was the refurbished original, as was the huge pine timber that spanned the length of the shop, serving as a countertop for the old-fashioned cash register and jars of candies. In the surface of the counter were carved the names of long-dead silver miners. The kindly proprietor, obviously very proud of the place, showed us around the rest of the store and into what had been and would be the poolroom. It was furnished with a real slate pool table and a tall cabinet that hid a fold-out Murphy bed.

Gary thought he recognized the proprietor's deep resonant voice, prompting us to ask his name. Gary was right. It was Lorne Saxberg, one of the CBC Radio broadcasters we had conversed with during our weekly phone-in on our cross-Canada trip. Small world, we thought, as Lorne carried on with an enthusiastic description of the Store's grand reopening in Silver Islet. It had taken several years of patient persuasion to convince the previous owners that he and his family sincerely intended to maintain the building and enhance the history of the place. For ten years the doors had been closed, so it was no wonder that any efforts on the part of the Saxberg family to keep the reopening quiet were doomed to failure. Lorne hadn't even had time to mark prices on anything when people began streaming through the door thanks to the efforts of two young town criers on bicycles who streaked up and down the Avenue shouting "The Store is open! The Store is open!"

At dusk, we walked the Avenue past windows aglow with candlelight and kerosene lanterns. We crossed a bridge and made our way to a small graveyard at the back of a field. It was a peaceful place marked with wooden crosses and engraved headstones. Thick, scaly trunks of aged spruce trees filled the oblong plots outlined with wrought-iron fencing where long ago, tiny seedlings had been planted to mark Anishnabe graves.

Very early the next morning, before the sun's first rays had burned off the thin wisps of mist, we paddled away from Silver Islet. In Tee Harbour, below the Sleeping Giant, a peregrine falcon came swooping down the talus slope toward us. On swordlike wings, it gave a spectacular aeronautical display. We felt immediately compelled by the high-pitched shriek to climb to those lofty heights for a peregrine's perspective of Lake Superior. Without exchanging a word, we angled the canoes toward shore and landed. Grabbing camera equipment and binoculars, we scrambled up the slope to the base of the cliff. From here, we thought we could see a chimney route up between two walls. Higher and higher we went until at last we stopped and turned to face the lake.

The view was like a great big living map. Off to the west beyond Pie Island were the gargantuan mounds of the Nor' Westers, to the south the elongated shape of Superior's largest island, Isle Royale, and to the east, the wide sweep of blue water. The sheer vastness made it impossible not to imagine we were overlooking the ocean. The distant waters speckled with freshening whitecaps resembled an Arctic sea filled with ice.

Eleven thousand years ago these would have been icebergs split off from a mile-thick ice sheet that lay just to the north and east of us. We could imagine how, long ago, the forested land around the Nor' Westers was an open tundra of swaying grasses, dwarf birch and scrub willow alive with roaming inhabitants. In this same season as we were now in, migrating ribbons of barren-ground caribou may have been settling into their northern calving grounds for the summer.

In fog, storm or wind it is easy to understand how Isle Royale, Superior's largest island, has exacted such a heavy toll on ships attempting to navigate around its tentacle-like reefs.

Lacking the keen eyesight and patient gaze of the early hunters, Gary and I peered around with binoculars. I shivered as a sudden chill breeze swept over the cliff edge. How would the hunter clad in animal skins have interpreted this wind? Maybe the response to such forces was instinctive, as natural as breathing. So many questions came to mind of how it would have been to understand the land so intimately, in so many dimensions. Carefully we descended the chimney and treacherous slope of sharp angled rocks, arriving safely back to the water's edge and our canoes.

By late afternoon, we had traversed Thunder Bay, hoping to make camp on the far shore. We imagined what a grand sight it would be from our tent door, the Sleeping Giant illuminated by the pink glow of the setting sun. The gulls of Caribou Island spotted us as we passed close to their small nesting colony. They rose in a blizzard of white wings. Each bird moved so perfectly within the flock, as if they were giant snowflakes being swept up by the rushing wind of a winter storm. Below the aerial din of shrieking, diving birds, their newly hatched and still flightless chicks scurried to and fro, hiding behind rocks and any bit of vegetation the rocky island provided. We laughed, pointing at the fuzzy gray bodies that had only their heads hidden from view. A short while later we camped on the mainland.

The next morning, we awoke to hear distant human sounds — voices, small engines and pounding hammers — joining the medley of bird song. We readied the canoes, contemplating a day of travel along the Thunder Bay waterfront. On the northern outskirts of the city, cottages and homes clustered in a tight beaded string behind the sandy shore. The bay was shallow a long way out. Lengthy water-intake pipes running from the dwellings into the lake either lay on the bottom heavily weighted with chain and cement tubes or they floated freely. The wake from a small motorboat cruising by caused the floating pipes to writhe around our canoes like huge black water snakes. The natural shoreline gradually succumbed to human influence. Concrete walled harbors and docks replaced the soft contours of sand spits and rocky bays. Waves eroding the banks carried sediment of unknown composition in bands of purple and brown that formed stripes across the blue water. When we stopped to stretch our legs, we looked with disgust at the oily film that ringed the canoes at the waterline. Only a few generations ago, the water here was pure enough to drink.

Near the city, the air grew warmer, and gathered a range of unpleasant urban smells. We paddled behind the long breakwalls that form a barrier between the lake and the harbors. By mid-morning, we had arrived at the tall red and yellow grain elevators of the Saskatchewan Wheat Pool. Cargo ships dwarfed our canoes as we came alongside to watch their holds filling with prairie grains. Wheat, canola, barley and oats arrive by rail from the western provinces and are loaded onto ships here in Canada's busiest inland port.

On the city's south side, a wide river uncoils toward the lake. It makes a quick descent from its headwaters in the Quetico Highlands to become the Kaministiquia River below Dog Lake. Along its length, miles of whitewater foaming through deep faults and tumbling over spectacular falls such as Silver and Kakabeka were a form-idable obstacle to early travelers. Before merging with Lake Superior, the Kam, as it is locally known, splits around some low, flat, partly treed islands. (The other two delta channels of the Kam are named McKellar and Mission Rivers.) Less than two hundred years ago, the North West Company established their fur trading headquarters on one of these islands. A seasonal village supported the annual summer rendezvous of traders exchanging fur pelts from the Northwest with European trade goods.

Paddling upstream on the Kam River away from the lake, we passed the squat white shapes of million-gallon oil storage tanks. From the industrial complexes came a monotonous clamor: whistles, machines, the grinding and clanging of metal against metal. Below us, dirty brown waters coursed by. Warehouses, residences, and industries old and new lined the riverbanks. On one side a railway appeared to have unzipped the fabric of water and land. Several miles upstream from the delta, on the inside river-bend, a thick pipe spewed waste effluent from a pulp and paper mill straight into the river. High above us, a dingy cloud of sulphurous fumes pouring from a red-and-white smokestack fanned out across the face of Mount McKay and the ancestral home of the thunderbirds. Appalled by the sight, smell, taste and sound, we hurried on.

Winter tightening its grip at the crest of the Kaministiquia's Silver Falls.

Near Cloud Bay, a beaver-dammed tributary stream creates a small headpond. Although trees may die, in so doing, they create new habitat for many species. Kingfishers, kingbirds, hawks and songbirds appreciate the perches the dead branches provide. Woodpeckers feed on insects under the decaying bark. Merganser and wood ducks nest in the hollow cavities bored out by the woodpeckers.

Swallows swooped around the entrances to nesting holes that peppered the steep clay bank upstream from the mill. Just ahead of us, a kingfisher prattled noisily as it flew from one branch to the next. Willows, grasses, alders and wildflowers overhung the riverbanks. And flowing beneath it all, water, the seemingly simple yet exceedingly magical liquid that flows through every living thing.

An hour's paddle up the Kam brought us to Old Fort William, now reconstructed and relocated as a tourist attraction. From the native village outside the stockade to the fur-trading enterprise within, the costumed staff reenact daily life of the early 1800s. In one building we met red-sashed voyageurs hefting bales of fur pelts. In another, a craftsman melted spruce gum to seal the seams on an authentic birchbark canoe. In the Great Hall, two men portraying North West Company partners Simon McTavish and his nephew, William McGillivray, conversed about the price of fur. They acted their parts well, depicting two arrogant men who put single-minded pursuit of profit before human values, epitomizing the true character of the fur trade. The doctor's wife instilled a chilling touch of reality when she handed us carpentry-like tools and explained how her husband pulled teeth and amputated limbs. Disease, alcohol and crowded living conditions took their toll among the local native inhabitants and French voyageurs living outside of the stockade. Such images contrasted sharply with the colorful gift shop where we were treated to portraits and souvenirs immortalizing the men of the North West Company.

For 50 miles (80 km) south, the shoreline on our map resembled the edge of a leaf after being eaten by a caterpillar. Knobby high peninsulas ended in pencil-thin points running toward the northeast. The band of skinny islands following this same northeast axis extended almost all the way from Pie Island to Cloud Bay, offering us wind and wave protection from the big lake. Splashes of brilliant orange lichens and green mosses mottled the dark cliffs. There were terraced cobble beaches to walk on and tiny islands alive with the clamor of more nesting gulls.

Three days later we were paddling into Pigeon Bay, a place where the passenger pigeon once flew in numbers great enough to darken the skies. At the back of the bay, a river of the same name flows in. From its source in the Quetico Highlands, this ribbon of water forms part of the longest undefended international border in the world. Once past that invisible political boundary into the United States, we only thought of being in a different country when we heard a strong accent, bought supplies with a different currency, or noticed the state registration on a sailboat's stern. We camped that night on a cobble beach facing the Susie Islands. In the blue of twilight, a full moon rose over their silhouetted shapes. We could imagine the delicate Arctic plants flowering in rocky fissures along the shore:

Erosion-resistant lava ridges running on a southwest to northeast axis form the basis for Isle Royale National Park's extensive hiking trail system. On a late September backpacking trip, we saw many cow moose with calves and heard bull moose in rut. To avoid being trampled, we were often forced to sidestep quickly off the narrow trail as the big bulls lumbered by huffing and puffing like freight trains.

A playful red fox takes time out from a game of hide-and-seek with Gary in the tall grass at Daisy Farm on Isle Royale.

Sun rising through the mist over the Susie Islands near Grand Portage Bay. Due to the harsh weather and cooling effect of Lake Superior, these and other north shore islands harbor sub-Arctic tundra plants reminiscent of the life that existed at the edge of retreating glaciers 10,000 years ago.

Tenuous roots of the Little Spirit Cedar have been anchored in the fissures of lichen-splattered granite on Hat Point since the seventeenth century, when European explorers first set foot on the shores of Lake Superior. For us, old trees are living touchstones with the spirit that connects the past, present and future.

crowberry, eyebright, pearlwort, spikemoss, harebells and others. We had already noticed how these small Arctic plant worlds flourished best in places exposed to the harshest of conditions. They were a little touchstone to a time when this was a land of permafrost and short, hurried summers at the edge of the ice cap.

A high point of land juts into the lake, separating two crescent-shaped bays. On the tip of this point lives the Little Spirit Cedar. Gnarled and twisted, this wizened old cedar stands defiantly immovable from the bedrock out of which it has grown for centuries. Drifting there in our canoes, we listened to the stories the old tree had to share. Phantom brigades of huge birchbark canoes paraded by, before moving off around Hat Point into Grand Portage Bay. The vision dissolved and we were alone again, the only two canoes for as far as the eye could see.

Before taxes were levied on the fur traders by the Americans at the turn of the nineteenth century, forcing the North West Company to move north to the Kaministiquia River, the fur-trade route to the Northwest was via Grand Portage and the Pigeon River. The phantom canoes we had imagined at Hat Point were the *canots de maîtres*, the big freight canoes from Montreal paddled by eight to twelve men. Carrying 3-ton (2,700 kg) loads, they arrived in July to meet the smaller *canots du nord* carrying furs out of the Northwest. The exchange that took place at this North West Company field headquarters was the ingenious link that made possible a trade route spanning the North American continent. And the key to it all was the men who paddled the canoes. Some voyageurs were seasoned travelers while others were greenhorns, and few, if any, could swim. They were physically powerful, stocky men who paddled to the rhythm of their own singing. Out of fear and respect for the power of the spirits that controlled water and wind, they emulated the Anishnabe by leaving offerings of tobacco at places like the Little Spirit Cedar.

We spent part of the morning exploring the reconstructed stockaded Grand Portage fort before setting off on the historic 9-mile (14 km) trail to Partridge Falls. Long before the arrival of Europeans, aboriginal people established this path, which bypassed the numerous rapids, steep-sided gorges and falls of the lower Pigeon River. The land on which the fort stood was also the site of a generations-old encampment that the North West Company simply appropriated. Lying only 50 miles (80 km) inland and 700 feet (230 m) above the elevation of Lake Superior is the watershed divide between the waters flowing to the Atlantic and Hudson Bay. This trail was, and still is, the easiest link for canoeists wanting to reach those vast networks of canoeable waterways leading to the Arctic Ocean and Hudson Bay from Lake Superior.

We could feel the ghostly presence of voyageurs trotting past heavily laden with two or three 90-pound (40 kg) packs filled with flour, sugar, kettles, beads, muskets, lead shot, corn, tobacco and kegs of alcohol. Alexander Henry the Younger's Journal of 1799–1814 described the portage as being "very bad in some places, knee deep in mud and clay, and so slippery, as to make walking tedious." Plank walkways now elevated us above such obstructions. During the fur trade, attempts were made to replace men with oxen and horses but nothing worked as efficiently as the human beasts of burden.

Halfway to Partridge Falls, we met a kayaker traveling down from Ely, Minnesota. He had abandoned the effort of carrying his fiberglass craft and was now dragging it, fully loaded with equipment, across the portage trail. Sharp rocks were shredding off stringy bits of blue gel coat and probably several years of the kayak's life. After a few moments of conversation, we turned to leave, feeling like old friends as we wished each other safe travels. Unburdened by packs, we moved quickly over the trail, covering the rest of the distance to the Pigeon River and the 9 miles back to Grand Portage before nightfall. We lowered our canoes off the pier and paddled on a short distance before setting up camp on a cobble beach.

Along the western, or Minnesota, side of Lake Superior, the shoreline is very straight. On our map, we traced the blue spidery arms of more than sixty streams and rivers rushing down from the Sawtooth Mountains. River names like Brule, Cascade, Poplar, Onion, Temperance, Cross, Manitou, Baptism, Beaver, Split Rock, Gooseberry, Silver and Knife reveal the religious, spiritual, historical and practical character of the region.

Hiking up the established trails at the river mouths gave us a chance to stretch our legs and learn something of the rivers beyond what we saw from the lake. At the Brule, we climbed a steep path for a mile or so through the dark forest where boreal species of balsam, spruce, white cedar, birch and aspen prevailed. The trail led us past two of the Brule's waterfalls to the Devil's Kettle. From the dizzy height of a black cliff, we threw a couple of sticks into the current above the falls. They parted company as the current split around an island of basaltic rock. One rode the long shimmering cascade into the black pool below while the other disappeared into the growling vortex of white foam that boiled up from a huge smooth-walled cauldron of rock. Where, we wondered, did the river take that stick? What significance would the diverging river channels have held for the people who lived here long ago, whose physical and spiritual lives were a constant balance of forces? A place like this would not have gone unnoticed. Even now, by the well-worn look of the trail, it was a continuing source of fascination to the human imagination.

Our enthusiasm to hike would melt away with the increasing heat of afternoon. At the Temperance, we were overcome by the desire to leap off the rock wall that rose from the cola-colored river. The water flowing from the hills was so much warmer than Lake Superior. Quickly beaching the canoes, we scrambled to the top barefooted and, with whoops of ecstasy, threw ourselves off. We jumped in a few more times, and then lay on the sun-warmed rocks to dry out.

Between the Cascade River and Tofte lie the Sawtooth Mountains, a series of ridges folding one behind the other. They are part of the geologically old basin that cradles the relatively young freshwater ecosystem of Lake Superior. The building and eroding of mountain ranges, the accumulation of sedimentary layers, lava flows, pressures of water and heat, the intrusion of shallow seas and the collision of continents make up the chapters in this long geological story. And Lake Superior is one of the few places on Earth where you can collect parts of this deep geologic past in your pockets. Beginning more than three billion years ago, as the Earth's crust hardened, vast continental plates formed. In this part of the world, these basement rocks became a huge flat plain known as the Canadian Shield. On our journey around the east and north shores at the Montreal River, Agawa Bay and the Pukaskwa coast, we would be walking over and camping upon this eroded, fractured crust.

Framed by the lush greens of cedar and sumac, this river flowing from the Sawtooth Mountains looks almost tropical.

Only the exhilaration of flying could compare with the experience of skiing for unending miles across thin, clear ice.

The mountain-building period that followed created the two ranges whose granite cores can be seen today embracing Lake Superior's east and west shores: the Giants Range in Minnesota and the Algoma Highlands in Ontario. Iron laid down in the sediments from the eroding Giants Range was gathered up in the next uplift of mountain building, part of which remains as the Gogebic Range on the south shore.

A million years ago, the Keweenawan Age hit with a period of tremendous volcanic activity and shifting of the Earth's plates. An arc-shaped rift through Eastern North America weakened the Earth's crust. Massive volumes of lava pouring through the fissures further depressed the land, causing the salt-water seas to flow in. Alternate eruptions of lava and periods of cooling and erosion formed the sandwich of sedimentary and lava layers that are most obvious today in the ridges and valleys on Isle Royale. Other rifts, faults and volcanic intrusions formed the great diversity of landforms on the northwestern side of Lake Superior. The legacy left by those early lava flows are the steep-walled canyons, precipitous coastal cliffs and a labyrinth of caverns and caves that we were now on the threshold of exploring.

We threaded our canoes through entrances into mystic caves filled with piercing shafts of light that penetrated through windows in the rock both above and below the surface of the water. An arch of brown volcanic rock framed with orange lichens and shaped like a curling wave led us into a small bay where the Manitou River tumbles down into Lake Superior. Near the base of the falls was a cave where a strange cyclopean creature kept guard over one of the steepest of all rivers on this side of the lake. Scaly rock tripe growing on the blue-gray rock formed one eye and a craggy nose. The cave was a gaping mouth filled with a jumble of silver-gray driftwood teeth.

This melt-sculpted ice chunk resting on the unblemished surface begged the question "How did it get here?"

Canoeing into the caverns and underwater caves of the western shore, where windows of light poured in from above and below, we felt part of an older, more mysterious world.

One of the most intriguing aspects of travel by snowshoes or skis has been discovering birds and animals that neither migrate nor hibernate. More often than not their presence is revealed only by stories in the snow, crisscrossing tracks, blood and feathers, fur tufts and scat. With the aid of our camera's infrared remote device, we acquired a closer look at timber wolves. Seeing them roaming across a frozen bay on Lake Superior and on some inland lakes were unforgettable experiences.

We had been traveling for fifteen days the evening we beached our canoes in a cove south of Little
Marais. The tiny bay was contained by a wall of volcanic rock on one side and flat rocks imbedded with
circular patches of quartz crystals on the other. On
the hill overlooking the bay, we could see a house,
no doubt where the owners of this beach lived. I
walked up to the house and got permission from a
man named Vern to camp there. Since much of the
Minnesota shoreline is privately owned, this was our
usual routine on this part of the trip. At dark, Vern,
Terry and their two dogs came down from the house
with a container of freshly churned ice cream to
share with us. Our conversations led to an invitation
to visit the local environmental education center,
Wolf Ridge, the next day. Terry worked full-time
teaching educators how to incorporate the themes,
philosophies and practical knowledge of the natural
world into their lessons.

Wolf Ridge is the result of an ambitious dream that evolved out of the first Earth Day celebrations in the spring of
1970. A schoolteacher, Jack Pichotta, proposed an Earth Week. It proved so successful that he opened an environmental
learning center at one of the Job Corps camps established by former U.S. president Johnson near Isabella. Over a
seventeen-year period, the program developed and finally land was purchased near Finland, Minnesota, to build the
extensive indoor and outdoor facilities that we visited that day. Programs incorporate real-life learning by having
students stoke woodburning furnaces to heat the buildings, package recyclable materials, and assist with an acid rain
monitoring program. One teacher developed some innovative environmental learning projects including the smokestack
machine, which allows students to compare the acidity of sulphur emissions from stacks with and without limestone
scrubbers. Converted slide and movie projectors could take microscopic aquatic creatures that were sandwiched between
two glass slides and project their image onto the classroom wall. In one laboratory we found boxes containing labeled
animal feces and radio tracking collars for snowshoe hare studies. In another room, an artificial rock wall provided a
controlled setting for teaching the skill of rock climbing.

During our visit, some 240 Minneapolis students and teachers were in residence at Wolf Ridge for the week. We watched a group of students act out assigned roles as characters in the fur trade and people living in an Anishnabe village. Activities at Wolf Ridge balance a general science curriculum with outdoor activities, which, depending on the season, include canoeing on nearby Wolf Lake, climbing through the challenging ropes course, hiking and snow-shoeing. Cree, the center's 115-pound (52 kg) Mackenzie Valley wolf, is a full-time resident. Born in captivity, Cree's mission is to assist in educating the public about the fascinating yet highly misunderstood lives of wolves.

Our day ended with a slow berry-picking hike up Marshall Mountain where cedar waxwings flocked to feed on the abundant serviceberries. From the summit we had a good view of the cliffs and the hack boxes where biologists are encouraging peregrine falcons to nest in the area once again. After the Second World War, widespread use of the pesticide DDT diminished the peregrine population by interfering with the birds' reproductive capabilities. Despite its ban in Canada and the United States, DDT is still a serious threat to peregrines in their South American wintering habitat.

Further south, the shore was indented with more amphitheater caves, grottoes and tilted lava layers. The land grew dramatically higher as the massive volcanic headland of Palisade Head came into view. From a distance, we caught a glimpse of the Split Rock lighthouse perched 200 feet (60 m) above the lake. Once we had rounded the point north of the lighthouse, large air bubbles came popping up around my canoe. I recognized the red-and-white divers flag. The beach

We were fortunate to have a calm day for canoeing past the Palisade Head cliffs. Unlike the gull that stares down at us, we cannot just rise off the surface or duck under breaking waves. And it is not just the force of the waves marching in but also the reactionary waves bouncing off the sheer walls that can make the water exceptionally turbulent on a windy day.

Gary's photograph catches me trying to photograph a family of ducks that just crossed our path near the Gooseberry river mouth. The agitated hen flutters behind her flightless brood, corralling them to safety. With the furious beating of stubby wings and lightning-quick pedaling of tiny webbed feet, the ducklings hastily outdistance our canoes.

was strewn with a colorful array of diving equipment. Peering into the clear blue depths, I watched two scuba divers rise from the wreck of the *Edenborn*. Before the lighthouse became operational, many steamers, including the *Edenborn*, foundered off these cliffs in November storms. From 1910 until 1969, before the advent of sophisticated radar systems, the many ships that plied the waters with loads of iron ore and other cargo were entirely dependent on the lighthouses as essential navigation aids. Suddenly the divers broke the surface next to me, shivering and blue-lipped even though it was a hot day. Little wonder there are few survivors from Superior shipwrecks.

As we traveled further south, the temperature increased. We were less than a quarter of the way around Superior. The lake surface warmed, the parched earth felt like concrete, and the air was thick and heavy to breathe. Our noses burned and our lips cracked. Caterpillars were opening up the leafy canopy, making the forested hillside look as it did back in the month of April. The smoke from a hundred forest fires burning to the northwest stained the whole sky wine-red each evening. Escape from the heat was a jump away over the side of the canoe or in the shade of trees by the water's edge. I never realized before just how much I valued the wealth of shade provided by old trees, such as a grove of old white pines gathered on a privately owned spit near the Encampment River. We leaned back and let the canoes drift, resting our heads on the canoe packs stuffed in the storage space behind each of our seats. I let my gaze climb the massive trunk of one nearby tree, up and up into the long feathery arms that reached for the sky capturing the light. Bunched together in the upper canopy were long, seed-bearing cones. A red squirrel busily nipped them off. One by one they landed with a light thud, falling among the soft bed of needles on the forest floor.

Skiing into the Apostle Island caves was so utterly different from visits by canoe and kayak. The sucking and gurgling water, reflecting green on the reddish-brown rock, was now silent. Snow and ice reflected light into the darkest corners of each cave.

THE JOURNEY EAST

St. Louis River to Whitefish Bay

Late July

DARK ANGULAR SHAPES LOOMED THROUGH THE HUMID HAZE, TURNING THE CITYSCAPE INTO A STRANGE MIRAGE. Deep in the southwest pocket of the lake at the mouth of the St. Louis River lies Duluth. To the west of us, the land swept up to form Hawk Ridge. During the autumn migration, the thermals above these cliffs carry the greatest concentration of hawks of any migratory route in the continental United States. Homes and downtown businesses have been built on the grid of steep roads below Hawk Ridge. Drawing closer, we noticed how the shimmering heat waves, which had magnified the size of the harborfront from afar, dissolved into the color and form of individuals strolling the pier, feeding the gulls and picnicking in Canal Park.

A pier light marked the opening to the ship canal that led into the Duluth harbor. We paddled past, timing our entrance into the channel with the next rising of the liftlock bridge. A barrage of large boats suddenly appeared from both directions, filling the canal. They motored at half throttle, throwing unexpectedly steep wakes. These rebounded, doubled in size, off the canal walls. Our canoes bobbed around like a couple of red corks as we fought to keep our balance. Out of the corner of my eye, I could see tourists gathering to watch the boats go through. Some pointed and some waved. Among the curious and interested, I could feel the silent anticipation drawing them in. Were we going to tip or get hit by a boat? Where had we come from and where were we going?

Before the canal was built in 1871, the great sweeping spit running parallel with the mainland lay unbroken. In Sieur Du Lhut's journal of 1679, he named this part of the spit the Little Portage. Formed by the lake's own counterclockwise currents, the Minnesota Point stretches for 9 miles (14 km) west to east. Behind it lies a huge freshwater estuary and the mouth of the St. Louis River. With the growth of industry and the expansion of mining in the Mesabi Range, the estuary was transformed into a major Great Lakes shipping port. At that time, ships entered the estuary from the eastern end of the spit via Superior, Wisconsin, giving the rival city the advantage in attracting harbor commerce. So Duluth contracted a steam dredger that worked for months to cut a channel across the point. When it finally stalled in the frozen gravel, residents gathered with picks, shovels and dynamite to finish the job. The City of Superior had obtained a court injunction to stop the building, but by the time it was served, a steam tug was chugging through the ships'-width passage. Eventually the canal came under federal rule and the court battles were settled in Duluth's favor.

When we visited smaller communities, we just fastened the tarpaulins over the cockpits of our canoes and left them. But in larger places, we usually prevailed on the first kindly person we saw living near the water and asked permission to leave our canoes in their backyard until our return. We were soon off exploring the Duluth harborfront with its many walkways and nineteenth-century brown-stone buildings. In the Canal Park Maritime Museum, we met an ardent shipwreck historian who regaled us with tales of Great Lakes storms and shipwrecks. "This afternoon," he told us, "you paddled over the site of one of the most dramatic of all wrecks on the Lakes." He pointed to the water just outside the canal. It happened for all of Duluth to see and hear in November of 1905. The steel freighter *Mataafa* was towing a barge three-quarters her length, and both vessels were loaded with iron ore. The voyage for the lower Great Lakes had only just begun when the temperature and barometric pressure plummeted. Extremely foul weather moved in, plunging the ship into a howling white world and cutting the visibility to zero. For twelve hours the Captain pushed on while the storm worsened. At last the decision was made to go back, a decision that meant maneuvering the ship and its barge through a 180-degree turn in house-high waves. Our experience paddling canoes and kayaks in breaking surf makes us appreciate the danger of turning broadside. With good fortune and seamanship, the *Mataafa* returned. Approaching the canal, the freighter cut loose the barge and made for the harbor where the navigation light had already been swept away. But her luck ran out as her stern rose high on a huge wave, burying the prow in the lake bottom. The stern swung sideways, dropping in a thunderous crash on the north pier. Once sideways to the entrance, the ship was driven aground and pounded until she broke apart. Duluth residents watched with horror, but there was nothing anyone could do to help. When rescue boats finally reached the crew the next day, the bodies of nine men had to be chopped free from their icy tombs in the sunken stern.

Long ago, at a time when this corner of the lake peeped out from under the mantle of glacial ice, the St. Louis River flowed south, carrying the meltwaters into the Gulf of Mexico. Gradually, as the glaciers retreated north and the land rebounded from the pressure put upon it by the ice, the course of the St. Louis River reversed, carving out the sweeping valley and gorge upstream from Lake Superior. The St. Louis forms one of the lake's largest tributaries and a canoe route link with the Mississippi and the Gulf of Mexico. Curiosity to seek out, discover and experience places beyond our known boundaries is a universal quality of human nature. As travelers in canoes, we share a bond with those

Squaw Bay, on the west side of the Bayfield Peninsula, is part of the Apostle Islands National Lakeshore. When blessed with the good fortune of calm weather, traveling by kayak is a very exciting and intimate way to explore the cliffs and caves.

who have paddled over the waters before us. Every morning they greeted the lake, assessed the weather, water and wind, and then, if all was well, launched their canoes. With the tireless rhythm of a body physically conditioned for long-distance travel, these men and women could cover great distances in short periods of time. Our own journeys have broadened our imagination about human travel. We are always asking ourselves about the lives of people who traveled where we now do. What kinds of lives did they lead? Why had they come? Where were they going? Did they share our feelings of insignificance and vulnerability out here on the lake?

In the days before European exploration, maps were not made on flat sheets of paper. Places yet to be discovered were distant visions in the minds of dreamers. Without boundaries separating the physical and spiritual worlds, these worlds of equal reality captured the soft nuances of seasonal change, the voices of the forest and the wind. The messages were easily heard and understood.

Europeans recorded and recalled their histories in an entirely different way. For us, their written journals provided a wealth of fascinating perspectives, ranging from those who recognized the dignity of aboriginal people to those who saw only profit and commerce in abundant resources. In a zealous desire to save souls, missionaries learned native languages and made detailed observations about the very beliefs that they tried so hard to vanquish. There was Etienne Brûlé, Samuel de Champlain's prime scout, who led the procession of European interests into Lake Superior in the early 1600s. The partnership of Radisson and Des Groseilliers gave France and England the first comprehensive report of the vast profits to be made from the resources in the country surrounding this freshwater sea. There was Sieur Du Lhut, who pioneered the fur-trade route from Lake Superior to the Gulf of Mexico via the St. Louis River, and Peter Pond, who accomplished the same into the Athabasca country. But trade and commerce across the continent had been going on for thousands of years before Europeans arrived. Aboriginal people traded copper from Lake Superior for shells from the Gulf, obsidian from the southwest and many other treasures. It was not trade that was new, but the conquest of land and its life. The Englishman living across the ocean made no connection between his purchase of a beaver hat and the exploitation of a nation of people, their land and their culture.

An arching bridge over the St. Louis River hummed with a steady stream of vehicles traveling between Duluth, Minnesota, and Superior, Wisconsin. In the harbor, tugboats maneuvered oceangoing cargo ships into grain-loading facilities and other docks running alongside iron-ore railways. Marinas bristled with tall masts from dozens of sailing vessels docked or lying at anchor. At the eastern harbor entrance, we paddled out from the lee side of Minnesota Point and left the cities behind.

For two days, the land was low and sandy and the canoeing more peaceful as there was less road access to the lake. Deer tracks dimpled the beautiful beaches, especially at the mouths of the Amincon, Middle, Poplar and Bois Brule Rivers. We knew the Bois Brule to be a historic route to Lake Michigan via the wild St. Croix River.

At Port Wing, the curve of the Bayfield Peninsula carried us northeast to the Apostle Islands, where layers of shale and Pre-cambrian sandstone have been sculpted by the waves, wind and ice into caves, arches, columns and flowerpots. Smooth swells rolling in from the west pounded the red cliffs of Squaw Bay. The cavernous passages, deep, long and high enough for our canoes on a calm day, swallowed the waves with deep sucking and slurping sounds. Digestion complete, the water was belched back through the openings, emitting deep booming sounds that we had only heard before in caves along the ocean. Passing Raspberry and Frog Bays and Red Cliff Point, we paddled south through the West Channel and Basswood Island, where a pair of bald eagles were nesting. Through our binoculars we could see the small northern Wisconsin town of Bayfield buzzing with summer tourist activity. People strolled up and down the shaded streets lined with small shops, inns, restaurants, and residences and a few elaborate old Victorian homes complete with turrets and large porches. Sailboats going to and fro between the islands colored the bay like a sprinkling of wildflowers emerging from a great blue field.

Madeline Island, the largest and only populated island in the Apostles group, framed by sky and water, lay long and low 3 miles from the mainland. Mon-ing-wun-a-kawn-ing, the beautiful Anishnabe name for this island, honors the presence of the golden-breasted woodpecker, or as we know it, the yellow-shafted flicker.

Ice appears to pour out from a portal in the sandstone wall of an Apostle Islands cave like flowing honey.

Overflow water on spring ice with reflections of trees, at Raspberry Bay, Apostle Islands.

We were drawn here by the fascinating story of how the island became the final resting place in a several-generation western migration of the Anishnabe from the east coast. The story tells of seven prophets who made seven predictions for the future, one of which told their people to travel inland from the St. Lawrence Gulf to "a turtle-shaped island where food grows on water." For five hundred years after their arrival at this place where the wild rice grows, Mon-ing-wun-a-kawn-ing, the people flourished, pursuing less nomadic lives of fishing and agriculture. A harmonious spiritual and physical relationship with the natural world was acknowledged and respected as individuals were initiated into the rites of Midewiwin, a powerful medicine society.

We pulled our canoes up on a small beach near the public wharf on Madeline Island. Just across the road in the village of La Pointe was a collection of hand-hewn log buildings surrounded by a cedar log stockade similar to the kind described by William Whipple Warren in his 1852 account, *History of the Ojibwa Nation*. Over the door facing the lake was a rack of moose antlers and below it, a sign proclaiming this quaint group of buildings to be a museum. The buildings themselves were part of the museum, including a sailor's home at one end of a pioneer barn, the old town jail, and one of the last surviving buildings of the American Fur Company, which operated here from 1816 to 1845. The displays inside were a collage of artifacts from the lives of Anishnabe, eighteenth-century fur traders, nineteenth-century settlers, missionaries, hunters, trappers and fishermen. Green painted cases on log walls contained a variety of pipes made of clay, pipestone, soapstone and fine-grained sandstone. The bronze medallions presented to native chiefs from sixteenth-century French and English kings were real, not plastic replicas. There was a sign describing the journey of ninety-three-year-old Chief Buffalo, "Kitch-Wazke," when he

A chandelier of ice graces the ceiling of a cave in the Apostle Islands.

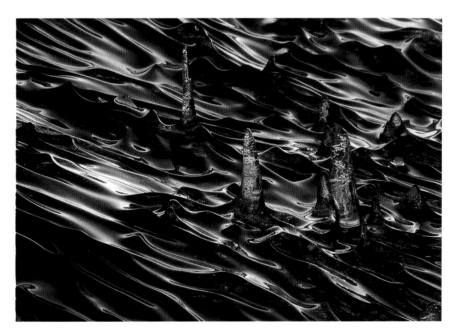

Flowing ice, Sand Island.

*While skiing through the Squaw Bay caves, we needed little imagination to turn the cavernous space
into a shark's jaw filled with row upon row of sharp teeth.*

Feeling like a little troll, I creep along an ice-walled cave.

On Sand Island, a tiny creek swollen by a cloudburst erodes the beach sand, creating the illusion of a sunset blazing behind a silhouetted ridge fringed with spruce trees.

traveled to Washington, D.C., to speak on behalf of his people's hunting, fishing and gathering rights on Lake Superior. Hand-printed cards explained various items in the cabinets: a pointy-bottomed Woodland Indian pottery vessel, golden thread medicine, a steel-and-flint firestarter in blackened buckskin, many pieces of pure float copper, a large copper pot, an Anishnabe headdress, brass and silver-plated buttons, pictures of old boats and early settlers, a maple sugar kettle, a spinning wheel and a handmade violin. An hour passed easily as we browsed through this one-of-a-kind museum.

After leaving the museum, we walked past a private harbor and into a grave site overlooking the lake. In the windswept grass we found unnamed and fenced graves of Anishnabe. White stones marked several graves that were nearly two hundred years old. Of the ones we could read, the family name

Masks of sand sculpted in several hours by the fingertips of waves.

Cadotte was chiseled into more headstones than any other. The name arrived with Michel Cadotte in 1793 when he came to set up a North West Company fur-trading post. Theresa Schenck, an anthropologist with a particular interest in the Anishnabe of Lake Superior, was there at the same time we were, trying to uncover any Anishnabe family history or archaeological information that would help prevent a marina development from happening on nearby Long Island. Her studies began with her great-great-great-great-great grandfather, John Baptiste Cadotte, who had maintained three fur-trading posts on the south shore. One of these was located on the island then known as St. Michel's Island. His son, Michel, married Madeline, daughter of Chief White Crane, and the island was renamed in her honor.

From the air, the pancakes-on-a-skillet-look of the Apostle Islands belies the close-up view of intriguing caves, grottoes and passageways carved into the soft sandstone. In the foreground lies Michigan Island, then Stockton, and to the distant left, the Bayfield Peninsula, off whose point are scattered a total of twenty-two islands.

Late in the afternoon, we set off across South Channel, intending to camp somewhere along Chequamegon Point. But the wind quickly changed our plans. When we were partway across, the wind swung around to the northeast. With no land for 250 miles (400 km) between us and the Pukaskwa coast, a blow from this direction meant a very rough crossing. I was thankful that we had lowered the seats and attached the tarps to the canoes before leaving Madeline Island. Running with these high waves, the canoes leapt forward like things possessed. They rose jubilantly on each wave crest, then rushed headlong with gleeful abandon into every wave trough. Crashing surf made the steep north-facing beach of Long Island an inhospitable place to land. We paddled west and parallel to the island, seeking a safer place to come ashore. With the waves now chasing us from the right rear quarter, I was extra

Warm air condensing over Superior's cold waters creates thick fogs that move in mysterious ways. There were times when we could only tell what the shoreline was like by the smell of the forest and the sound of water against sand or rock.

thankful for a rudder to keep the boat on course. Finally, the lighthouse on the west end of Long Island came into view, we rounded the point and the surface calmed.

A severe storm in November 1975 filled in the opening between Long Island and Chequamegon Point, creating one long barrier sand-spit. Behind it lies one of the largest freshwater estuaries in the world. It is unique among the Apostle Islands, and indeed is something quite rare on Lake Superior.

A scrubby mix of wildflowers, bullrushes, blueberries and poison ivy lining the shore pulsed with birdlife: bluejays, kingbirds, robins, cedar waxwings, song sparrows, red-wing blackbirds, killdeer and sandpipers. A lone black tern dove repeatedly into the bay while a bald eagle soared above the band of poplars and spruces threading the backbone of this peaceful habitat. Although we didn't see any piping plovers, Long Island is an important nesting area for this endangered species.

A crescent moon was rising by the time we set up camp below a sand dune, being careful not to squash the tangled ground cover of purple beach peas. Somewhere close by a sweet-scented shrub perfumed the air. While we were eating our supper and listening to the surf, Gary nudged me, pointing to the top edge of the dune. Moving soundlessly across the sand were the silhouetted shapes of three coyotes. For a while they yipped and barked and howled, increasing the sense of wildness we already felt on this island so full of life. Maybe the lights twinkling in the depths of Chequamegon Bay weren't Ashland at all, but the campfires of the Anishnabe gathered for a Midewiwin ceremony.

With 600 miles (1,000 km) behind us and a month of paddling under our belts, we were much less preoccupied with whether our bodies and equipment could withstand the rigors of the trip. We felt strong and conditioned. All the knots and aches in our muscles had long since been worked out. With each week that passed, our familiarity with the lake grew, and with it our confidence. The shoreline revealed more colors, expressions, animals and birds. Our binoculars helped us in matching various sparrows, thrushes and warblers with their songs. The hollow-drainpipe tune that heralds evening and time to make camp turned out to be a veery. A burbling stream of clear notes trilled again and again belonged to the tiny winter wren. And one of the most common was the high-pitched whistling call of cedar waxwings, darting out from the shore to catch insects on the wing. To our right side lay the details of shore, and to the left only water, stretching out to an unbroken horizon.

Wherever blueberries grew, we were there picking them, in the company of black bears and gulls. Maple sap, fiddlehead ferns, berries, fish and wild rice are some of the seasonal foods that we enjoy.

On a warm, hazy, silent sleepy sort of morning in Oronto Bay, the movement of a tiny dark speck far off in the distance caught my attention. I focused on the horizon, aware of how my depth perception gets distorted. I see floating gulls as freighters and bees as hummingbirds.

"I think it's a butterfly," I remarked, watching the rhythmic, undulating flight pattern, like a feather caught by the breeze.

"I think you're right," Gary said, lowering his binoculars. "Amazing, way out there."

The insect drew closer until we recognized the familiar orange–and–black pattern of the Monarch butterfly's wings. Orange as the lichens, black as the rock tripe, and as thin as the brittlest leaf. Moving steadily with purpose, those tiny wings had carried it across many miles of open water. We paused to watch with wonder as it broke the directness of its flight, fluttered around us, then moved off toward the land traveling much faster

From a profusion of white flowers carpeting the forest in spring comes the ripening of blueberries and bunchberries in August. Both are edible, although the delicate sweet blueberries are much preferred.

than our canoes. Such a delicate creature to follow a migration route that spans half a continent between Lake Superior and central Mexico's Sierra Madre, a distance far greater than all the miles we were paddling around Lake Superior.

Little Girls Point lies east of Saxon Harbor on the Michigan shoreline, a place well known to many agate hunters as a prime collecting beach. An elderly couple, the Omans, have lived at Little Girls Point most of their lives. Intrepid agate collectors, this pair has traded and purchased agates from all over North America. In fact, most of what was displayed in their tiny shop had been bought or traded for in the Southwest. We rested and talked with the Omans before heading back out on the lake.

A graying sky obscured the sun and a southeast wind sent worried lines rippling across the bay. Several cars were in the park, indicating that a scattering of agate hunters were still intent upon their work, busily digging, probing, selecting and discarding rocks. Some were on their hands and knees, heads buried as they dug furiously, like dogs digging for bones. Others had fashioned groundhog–like holes and mounds. Others were using special long–handled ladles to scoop

Lightning streaks the far horizon as a storm front stampedes toward us.

up rocks, saving their backs from all the stooping and straightening. One man, somewhat disenchanted with the process, had left his wife doing the digging and came over to talk to us. He felt obliged, as many people did, to tell us of the worst storm they had ever known on Lake Superior.

He was genuinely concerned as he cautioned us on the folly of our endeavor. He eyed our canoes with suspicion. I handed him my bentshaft paddle. I could see that the featherlight basswood wasn't going to inspire any more confidence. With no quick way to convince him of the safety inherent in our pursuit, nor a way to convey how we avoid confrontations with the lake, we merely smiled and waved before pushing off from shore. To us, our journey was easy compared to that of the Monarch butterfly, but to that man we were the butterfly about to be swept up by the wind and swallowed by the waves.

The Porcupine Mountains seemed to crouch in defiance of the dense fog that curled in off the lake. Rolling over the hills and swallowing up points of land, the fog drew close enough to send its cold breath circulating down inside my canoe. I shivered, feeling as if I had been immersed in the lake itself. Just then, the inside bottom of our canoes turned deathly cold. We backed up and then went forward until we found a distinct line between the warm and cold waters. The sensation reminded us of crossing a thermocline while scuba diving in northern lakes. (A thermocline is a distinct horizontal line dividing the warm, circulating surface and the cold, still depths.) The phenomenon we were experiencing is called a thermal bar. Although they are rare on lakes, Superior is big enough that the deep, cold offshore waters take much longer to warm up than the shallow, near-shore waters, resulting here in a distinct vertical temperature change dividing the two. As the

Flowing beneath the crouched shape of the Porcupine Mountains is a river called Presque Isle. Paddling a short distance upstream from the lake, we discovered a fantastic display of kettles. These smooth circular depressions form when a river tumbles rocks in one place for a very long time.

Golden birch leaves and pine needles speckle the layers of shale on the Presque Isle River.

summer progressed, this wall would move further from shore. It has a significant effect on underwater life and the breeding cycles of wetland species.

As we rounded the point into Sleeping Bay, two eagles circled the oldest and largest of the white pines that grew between the East and West Sleeping Bay Rivers. We could make out a nest and the hunched shape of a young eagle perched on an outstretched limb. The eagle turned its head slowly and deliberately, appearing to watch the aeronautical display of its parents with dispassionate interest. Over the lake, bruised purple clouds weighed heavily on the horizon, squashing the red sun into a shape resembling an overripe tomato. A storm was rolling in. We made camp quickly on one end of the long beach as far from the eagle's nest as possible. Soon clouds like great humped buff-aloes came thundering across the open prairie of the lake. Lightning sparked through holes, forming deep-set luminous eyes. Rain caught on the wind was the dust rising from their pounding hooves. Just as we made for the shelter of the tent, the herd split in two. Part of it moved on to the southeast while the other rumbled off to the southwest of Sleeping Bay, leaving us to gaze upon a clear night sky with only the sound of the dying wind. Sleeping Bay was going back to sleep and I wondered if the young eagle felt relieved.

Poking up into Lake Superior, like an otter's head peering above the waves, is the broad curving arm of the Keweenaw Peninsula. Along the tip, in a series of ridges, sheer cliffs fall to sweeping valleys. In the center of the peninsula, an ancient rift cutting across this landform creates the basin for a long, narrow lake. Portages used to be made around the marshes on each end until a canal, dredged out for boat traffic, effectively made the east end of the peninsula an island. We debated whether to canoe around the outside of the peninsula or across the traditional, more protected inland route to Keweenaw Bay. Finally, we settled on just getting to the Coast Guard station at the opening to the Ship Canal and Portage Lake. From there, we would let the wind decide.

Making camp in Sleeping Bay on the first of August while swirling clouds from the north and east gather with ominous rumblings.

Portaging across a black stamp sand beach near Redridge. In the nineteenth century, stamping mills crushed the ore in the process of obtaining the copper. The excess rock spewed into Lake Superior was carried by the counterclockwise current, depositing it further east along the Keweenaw Peninsula shoreline.

We camped about 10 miles (16 km) east of the station near Redridge, on a strange black sand beach. The texture of the flat, shiny grains was unlike any sand I had ever let run through my fingers. Some children from a nearby cottage were attempting to build castles, but the sand would collapse instantly into a conical pile. As we later discovered, the black beaches followed the natural lake current all the way along the outside edge of the Keweenaw Peninsula.

Gary paddled up alongside me the next morning and whispered that he felt as if we were tiptoeing, trying not to wake the Giant. But alas, even the quiet splashing of our paddle strokes was too loud. The wind stirred the lake to a white–capped chop, just allowing us time to slip behind the breakwall and into the Ship Canal. After a few miles, we entered Portage Lake. The rolling hills and farmland was more rural than anything we had yet seen immediately along Superior's shoreline. We spent a couple of hours exploring Houghton and picking up some supplies, and then we crossed the river to view the crumbling copper mines below Hancock at Ripley.

Small streams flow off the Keweenaw Peninsula, a huge finger of land that juts into the heart of the lake.

The area around the Keweenaw has seen the rise and fall of the world's most extensive copper mining. In the mid-nineteenth century, American industry craved copper to make brass, an alloy of zinc and copper. Douglas Houghton, Michigan's first state geologist, surveyed the Upper Peninsula for copper, and his findings stirred excitement. Not long after 1827, a fur trader named Julius Eldred gained the confidence of Keatanang, the chief of the Ontonagon band, whom he persuaded to trade away the Ontonagon Boulder. This mass of pure copper had long been revered by the Anishnabe as a manitou. Eldred purchased it with "two yards of scarlet cloth, four yards of blue cloth, two yards of every colour in silk ribbons, thirty pairs of silver earrings, two new white blankets and ten pounds of tobacco." (From *Kitchi-Gami: Life*

In autumn, sugar maple leaves colour Brock Mountain and the rest of the Keweenaw Peninsula.

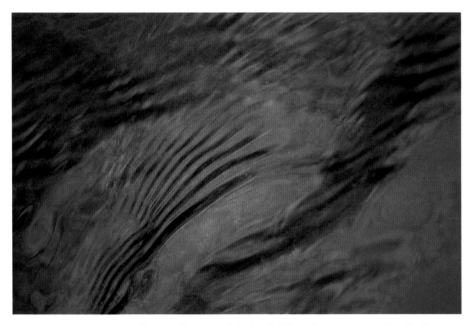

In the reflections of the Eagle River, Gary saw spreading feathers and a flurry of beating wings.

Among the Lake Superior Ojibway, by Johann Georg Kohl.) With a prayer to the Great Spirit, Keatanang then offered all this to the river and permitted Eldred to load up the copper and paddle it far away. The incongruous home of the Ontonagon Boulder is now a slick showcase in the Smithsonian Institute in Washington, D.C. By 1842, the Treaty of La Pointe had been signed and these lands were forced open for copper mining. Over the next fifty years, the copper boom drew thousands of people north to the Upper Peninsula.

We bucked stiff headwinds but made the best of the next day, enjoying the feeling of protection that came from having land on each side of us. Bullrushes on the edge of Portage Lake were flowing and weaving in the wind like long hair. Intermingled with the rushes was a mass of purple loosestrife. The alders and other shrubs were alive with twittering yellow warblers, kingbirds and a few blue herons. We camped in a field near Chassel where the high winds finally brought rain.

The next morning, under blue skies spotted with cumulus clouds, we paddled into Portage Entry, but west winds let us go no further. This two-day blow felt to us as if it would continue for another two days. We decided our trust in the wind and our decision not to canoe around the peninsula at this time had been a good one. Already we had met several families between Houghton and Chassel who shared stories, places of local interest and current events in Keweenaw news. In Portage Entry, an elderly couple walking on the street began talking with us and before we knew it, we were at their kitchen table. Over tea and Korpu, a thin Finnish crispbread, the Heikkinens described their early years on the Keweenaw. Lempi had come from a fishing family and Henry had worked in the copper mines. When we asked about the black beaches, he explained how they resulted from copper mining.

He explained that the ore was brought down from Painsdale in railroad cars and delivered to the stamping mills at Freda and Redridge. He described the 1,000-pound (450 kg) stamps that were used to crush the rock and how a chemical process caused the copper to float so it could be skimmed off the top. "The copper was sent on to Quincey, Lake Linden and Hubbell on the Keweenaw," Henry said, "while the excess crushed rock and chemical mixture was just spewed into Lake Superior. The east-flowing current carried the crushed rock along the shore for many miles. Storm waves have played their part in creating the huge black beaches."

Beyond Portage Entry, the shoreline runs almost straight south for 4 miles (6 km) to the village of L'Anse and then turns northeast for 5 miles (8 km) out to Point Abbaye, forming a big triangle, the throat of Keweenaw Bay. For the first part of the morning, we paddled in close to the black and red shale buttresses where thin, silver streams poured into the lake. There was a constant clatter of small stones tumbling down the eroding cliffs.

We paddled down into Keweenaw Bay until the far shore was a reasonably safe distance for us to cover. "Let's make for that tower," Gary suggested. As we drew closer, the letters spelled out FORD. Later we discovered that this had once been a Ford factory manufacturing wooden parts for Model T cars. In those days, Ford cars sported wood paneling inside and out, wooden window trim and even wooden wheel spokes.

After we reached the south side of Keweenaw Bay, a breeze began picking up out of the northwest. Knowing it would only increase, we began looking for a beach to surf up on safely. The wind was once again setting the day's itinerary for us. So many times it was the wind that blew us ashore at just the right moment to find a special campsite, sight an animal, discover an old cabin or meet new friends. I wondered if these coincidental occurrences might be the lake's way of acting as our tour guide.

On that afternoon the first sand beach appeared to be on private property. There was a sauna house down by the shore and a low white cottage nestled beneath the hemlocks and pines. An excited chocolate-colored Lab came bouncing down the beach. Its owner, with an equally exuberant personality, came over to greet us. He wore a pair of polished brown shoes, flannel pants and a shirt buttoned neatly to the top. The smile that spread over his round, jolly face seemed to be constantly on the verge of laughter.

"Hello, I'm Fred Waisenen." He took my hand in a firm grip. After introducing ourselves, I asked if we might just wait out the wind a bit. Fred seemed pleased. By this time his family had joined us down on the beach. They were all asking questions and looking at the canoes with great interest.

"You know, come to think of it," said Christine, Fred's daughter, "in all the years I've been here, you two are the first people that the lake has washed up on our beach without needing to be rescued." She soon had us all laughing with tales of the mishaps of previous visitors while Fred encouraged his dog, Shoe, to prance around on his hind legs.

Before we knew it, the Waisenens were leading us up to the cottage. On the way, we had a tour of the finest wood-fired sauna we had ever seen, and we had seen plenty of them! Several generations ago, Finnish immigrants, struck by the similarity of Lake Superior to their homeland, had settled on the southern and western shores from Marquette to Thunder Bay. They made a living fishing. To the Finns, a sauna is a pleasant ritual. We would easily agree. Jumping into the cold waters of Lake Superior after soaking up the heat was a fine feeling indeed. Inside the cottage, the low ceiling, pine-paneled walls lined with books, and windows sectioned off in little squares with views to the lake reminded us of other multi-generation summer cottages we had visited where stories seem to exude from the walls themselves.

Fred welcomed us in and seated himself in his favorite chair in the corner of the room. Helen served coffee and a selection of Cornish pasties that were left over from the big family reunion the day before. Soon the maps were out and the conversation bounced from the history of Point Abbaye to our own adventures on the lake, to the Aura Jamboree, an annual fiddle festival organized by the Waisenens, to the controversial subject of the proposed pulp and paper mill at Arnheim near Portage Entry.

"Coming from Canada, you must be familiar with pulp and paper mills," said Fred.

Nodding in agreement, we were reminded that all the people we had met since entering Portage Lake had managed to weave the topic of the proposed mill into conversation with us. It was the familiar dilemma of industry jobs versus the protection of the natural environment. In a region well acquainted with the boom-and-bust economic cycle of harvesting resources, there were many people who put a high value on clean air and clean water. There were native people, Finlanders, and back-to-the-landers from the urban south. A grassroots environmental group called FOLK, the Friends of the Land of the Keweenaw, emerged to oppose the mill. Industry relies on the word "jobs" as a powerful carrot to persuade people, but it also relies upon public ignorance of the issue. When the local newspaper began publishing in-depth editorials and FOLK put forward educated arguments showing how the long-term economic health of the region depended upon their forests and clean water and air, public opposition to the mill grew. Plans to diversify local manufacturing, to reduce the need for bright white chlorine-bleached paper, and to employ forestry practices that maintain healthy forests were the kinds of solutions being talked about in the Keweenaw Peninsula, thanks to the efforts of FOLK.

Lovely long beaches gracing the lakeshore below the Huron Mountains lured us ashore the next day for lunch and a swim. While lying in the shade of an old white birch, we watched three whitetail deer step cautiously out from the forest edge. Ears twitching, black noses raised to catch unusual scents, the deer finally decided the coast was clear and began browsing their way toward us. We remained motionless. It wasn't until they were within several feet of us that the buck suddenly snorted and turned, kicking up his hind legs. His white tail flashed as a warning to the others. Without even knowing the danger, the does bounded down the beach and back into the forest.

Just as we were coasting away from shore, Gary spotted a log cabin about halfway down the beach. They attract us like iron to a magnet. We followed the beach to a place where the Pine River enters Lake Superior. Angling our canoes into the

The Pine River that flows from the Huron Mountains is part of a watershed protected by the dedicated efforts of several generations of private landowners.

current, we sprinted up the shallow S–bend and into the calmer waters. Both sides of the river were flanked with sturdy old log cabins weathered to the color of driftwood, blending perfectly with the surroundings. Just then, a beautiful green cedar canvas canoe slid out from one of the log boathouses.

I asked if this place had a name, and the man in the canoe answered with a smile, "The Huron Mountain Club."

We reacted with surprise. Local people had mentioned the club and Grace Lee Nute's book on Lake Superior also described it, but for some reason, we had both imagined it to be somewhere back in the mountains, not down on the lakeshore. Almost a century ago, this land had been purchased by wealthy industrialists to form a hunting and fishing club. Their wish was to preserve some of the only remaining virgin forest left in the clearcut Upper Peninsula. Over the years, the club increased its membership and acquired more land so that it now owns the entire Huron Mountain watershed.

White-tailed deer moved north in the nineteenth century, occupying the disturbed forest created by loggers. Today they are the most populous ungulates in the Lake Superior region, partly as a result of the decline in timber wolves, their primary natural predator. We crept up on this small group on a beach near the Huron Mountains.

It was here at the club that we first met Fred Rydholme, a born storyteller. He tells humorous and imaginative stories in a deep, captivating voice that we could listen to for hours. A wealth of historically accurate details are woven into tales that always end in thought–provoking ways. For almost twenty years, he and his wife June ran the children's program at the club. When Fred invited us out to his cabin on the Yellow Dog Plains to the south, we accepted without hesitation. On the way out, Fred described his first days exploring the Huron Mountains after the club hired him to fill wood and ice boxes. He remembered being out on Mountain Lake with the rocky cliffs of the Huron Mountains rising before him, thinking how much forethought, money and perseverance it had taken to save this place from the ax, saw and bulldozer. He loved traditional wooden rowboats and canoes. Out on the lakes, there was no noise, no bad smells and no motors.

When Fred and June purchased their parcel of 80 acres (32 ha) on the Yellow Dog Plains in 1949, nothing but knapweed, asters and St.-John's-Wort dotted the wasteland of enormous stumps where thousands of immense red and white pines once grew. That year Fred and June, with the help of a Boy Scout troop, planted two thousand trees. These pines are now part of the 960–acre (390 ha) area honored as the oldest continuous tree farm in Michigan. But tree farmer seemed an unlikely title for Fred. The weathered lines across the brow of his kind, smiling face deepened as he reached down to gently stroke the feathery needles of a pine seedling. "So little is known about replanting and growing white pine," he said. "The logging companies want trees so fast they are turning forests into farms." Fred should know better than most about raising young trees of different species. He and his wife have planted more than a quarter of a million of them. "Most people think of jack pines as small and gnarly with tight little cones," he said. "In the 1930s, there were forests of jack pine a hundred and thirty feet tall here on the Yellow Dog Plains."

Back in the cabin, I curled up in a seat fashioned from the hollowed–out burl of a huge basswood tree, feeling like a hibernating raccoon. Every object in Fred's cabin had a story, from the logger's peavey hook growing from the middle of the coffee table to the panoramic camera that hung from the ceiling, and the huge chunks of oxidized turquoise–blue copper. Long into the night, we shared thoughts and theories about human travel and trade along Lake Superior's shores several thousand summers ago.

From Granite Point to Sugarloaf Mountain just north of Marquette, a day and a half away from Fred's cabin, the sight of granite rock recalled familiar and treasured places to canoe. For the first month of the trip, we saw layers of lava and sandstone covering Precambrian granite, the rock type we

Skiing along the edge of Grand Island, the largest island on Superior's south shore,
we were awed by the massive icicles clinging to the sandstone cliffs.

would see along the eastern and north shores. Among the oldest of rocks, this granite forms the basement to continents and oceans. It is a rock that speaks of the planet's earliest era, a time before rivers, lakes, oceans and life.

For the next 35 miles (56 km), from Marquette to Au Train Bay, strange winds gusted from all directions, producing troublesome waves. Our canoes wallowed around like drunken sailors, until our stomachs felt queasy. Storm clouds formed and lightning chased us from the lake several times, but it never rained. That night we pitched our tent opposite Grand Island at Munising and contemplated the following day with some reservation. The cliffs would be a formidable barrier to safety if the winds came up as suddenly as they had today. We fell asleep praying for fine weather.

Crossing the mirror-calm bay at dawn, we reached the great sandstone walls. They rose above us, curving off into the distance. We could never have imagined such colors. Glazed with water gently percolating from the sandstone, copper, limonite, and iron minerals formed magnificent striped draperies. Unreal in their varnished brilliance, the colors of rose, turquoise, ink black, ochre, pearly white, burnt sienna and rust red streamed down the cliff face. I paddled into the shade between the mineral striped walls and the line of water droplets that sprinkled down from the upper edge of the scalloped cliff. From here I could dip my fingers into the natural pigments that pooled along the narrow shelves. The deck of my canoe became my canvas. In that one day between Munising and Grand Marais along the Pictured Rocks National Lakeshore, we paddled for 40 miles (60 km) below sandstone cliffs of many colors and amphitheater-like caves so huge that a hundred other canoes could have shared the space with us. We plucked agate rocks from

I could hear, and in places see, the water rushing down inside these hollow pillars of ice.

Grand Portal Point. Lake Superior blessed us with an incredible day for exploring the caves and cliffs of the Pictured Rocks National Lakeshore.

Brilliant striped curtains of oxidizing minerals pour down the walls at the Pictured Rocks.
When I dipped my fingers into the colors that had pooled along the ledges they were stained as if by paint on a palette.

Telemark skiing down the powdery flanks of the Grand Sable Dunes during a winter ski camping trip along the Pictured Rocks National Lakeshore.

knobby columns and marveled at how a great old pine kept a firm hold on life from the top of a flowerpot formation. A single thick tree root anchored it to the mainland, much like a boat tied to shore. Ordinarily we might have camped right here, but we decided to make the most of the perfect weather conditions and paddle on another 20 miles (32 km) to Grand Marais.

Miles and miles of white sand beach stretched all the way to the lighthouse on Au Sable Point. Beneath us, hardened sand created a maze of wormwood patterns on the lake bottom. Gary was some distance out front and by the time I reached the lighthouse, he had already disappeared around the point. My next sight of him came as a complete surprise. Ahead, the tiny red sliver of Gary's canoe was framed against a towering backdrop of sand dunes unlike anything I had ever seen before.

We edged our canoes around the last point into the deep-water harbor of Grand Marais. Tunes from a nearby bluegrass festival serenaded us across the bay, creating the perfect ending to the perfect day. It was August 12 and we had reached the halfway point in our 2,000-mile (3,200 km) journey.

Broad beaches of sand and gravel, backed by forests of spruce, cedar, birch and hemlock stretched eastward 40 miles (60 km) to Whitefish Point. The lay of land caused the two main rivers, Blind Sucker and Two Hearted, to flow in a peculiar fashion, parallel to the beach, for several miles before carving an opening out to the lake. When the light, puffy clouds began foaming up like bubble bath, we expected an afternoon storm. Uncertain gusty winds swirled the sand into tiny tornadoes that whipped the grains against our skin and eyes. The first jagged bolts of lightning arched from cloud to cloud, shooting electricity in all directions. Bowling balls of thunder bounced across the alleys of darkened sky. With such a wide expanse of beach separating us from the protective forest, we were very exposed. The rain was falling as a white sheet as we leapt from the canoes and hauled them a safe distance from the water. Quickly we fastened the tarpaulins

Learning to judge the weather is an important aspect of journeying on Lake Superior. Paddling below these pebbled pillars and walls of Pictured Rocks would be an entirely different experience in high winds and waves.

An unbroken stretch of white sand between Beaver Lake and the Hurricane River, known as Twelvemile Beach, might well pass as the Bahamas until you dip your hand into the cool waters of Lake Superior.

*A magical ending to a 40-mile (64 km) day from Munising to Grand Marais, passing the Pictured Rocks,
Twelvemile Beach and the Grand Sable banks and dunes.*

and dashed for the woods. There was a moment of hesitation as I ducked beneath the tall pines, remembering an evening a few years back when Gary and I watched a bolt of lightning blow a pine tree into kindling sticks. Then thunder crashed through my thoughts, sending me into the woods as fast as I could run. Large fat drops drummed the bunchberry leaves as Gary popped up the umbrella and we crouched like a pair of mice under a mushroom. From our tiny dry space, we peered out at the rain cascading off the umbrella in a waterfall all around us. I reached into my pocket for a chocolate bar while Gary recited an umbrella's list of attributes on a trip: "A sail in the wind; a sunshade for equip-ment and food, a sunlight reflector and diffuser for photography, a cover for cameras and people in the rain..."

"How about a lightning rod?" I added.

The deluge continued for ten minutes, and then diminished to a light shower. Confident it

A day's paddle upstream from Whitefish Bay, the golden cascade of the Tahquamenon River's Upper Falls spills over the lip of a sandstone cliff.

had passed, Gary folded up the umbrella and we marched back down to the canoes. But just as I began undoing my tarp, a bolt of lightning streaked across the sky, followed by an explosive crack. Had we been dogs, our tails would have been tucked between our legs as we bounded back to the woods. Three times this happened, the final deluge catching us in the midst of launching our canoes.

"Okay, you win!" I called out. Then suddenly, in a perfectly timed response, the sun peaked out beneath the storm clouds. The golden light split into a full spectrum of colors as it shone through the water vapor, arching over in a brilliant double rainbow.

After two long days of travel and a morning's paddle across Tahquamenon Bay, we had to call it quits. The whitecaps of Whitefish Bay lay between us and Gros Cap. We beached the canoes on a stony beach, hoping the landowner would give us permission to camp. From the top of the bank, I crossed an expansive lawn to a two-story house. A man

Clouds hurrying past the face of the moon. On our eighty-day journey, the sun was our clock and the phases of the moon our calendar. One of the three full moons was a full eclipse.

answered my knock at the door. Without giving him time to object, I explained our predicament and asked if he minded us camping. The edges of his mouth turned up. "Well, I can't hardly send you back out on the lake now, can I?"

He held out his hand, introducing himself as Raymond. "You might as well come up for some coffee. You are in luck. It's fresh today."

A few minutes later, I returned with Gary. Raymond answered our quizzical stares at thirty one-gallon jugs of coffee covering all the countertops and kitchen table. "I don't like making coffee so I only do it every three months. I keep the jugs in the freezer." He put the pile of used coffee filters and a huge, empty coffee tin into the garbage. He filled three cups and then disappeared into another room. We heard a sound like rocks clattering on shore and then he returned with a plate of Fig Newtons. He motioned us through to the living room. A huge picture window filled the wall that faced the lake. Every tree in the garden had been pruned of its lower limbs so as not to impede the view.

"Grab a seat." Raymond indicated a selection of three-legged milking stools scattered around the room. "I bought a kit for one and enjoyed making it so much, I ordered ten more." In the middle of the bare room, surrounded only by other milking stools, we huddled around the map of Lake Superior sipping coffee.

Raymond seemed pleased to have company. He took us on his Sunday afternoon bicycle route to a high bluff where we had a wonderful view of Whitefish Bay, Iroquois Lighthouse and Gros Cap across the bay, and he showed us the Iroquois Lighthouse museum.

For dinner we perched on our milking stools and ate TV dinners. For dessert, he handed us each a knife, fork and a banana on a plate. Raymond stabbed his with the fork. It shot off onto the floor. I tried to slice mine but the rock-hard banana just skidded off the plate and landed in my lap. Gary gave up on the implements and ate it like a Popsicle.

"A sale on bananas last year," Raymond explained matter-of-factly.

Very early the next morning, while all was still dark, we crept down the stairs, determined to cross Whitefish Bay before the wind came up. Raymond was already in the kitchen microwaving a jug of frozen coffee. He followed us down to the beach, encouraging us to return if it proved too rough. In a practiced pattern, we loaded the canoes and launched them into the gently rolling swell of Whitefish Bay.

Superior's great expanse deters lake crossings by hawks, eagles and falcons. Red-tailed hawks like this one on the hills above Iroquois Point are among the thousands of birds of prey that migrate north and south over Whitefish Point and Duluth's Hawk Ridge.

In autumn, the forests of the eastern shore blaze red, orange and yellow. These sugar maple trees are among the most prolific of the deciduous species. In spring, we regard the flow of sap as a celebratory beginning to a new season. The sap is tapped from the trees and boiled down to make maple syrup.

THE JOURNEY NORTH

Whitefish Bay to the Michipicoten River

Mid-August

TWO POINTS OF LAND MARK THE HEAD OF THE ST. MARY'S RIVER AT WHITEFISH BAY. FROM IROQUOIS POINT on the Michigan shore, we had a 4-mile (6 km) crossing to reach Gros Cap on the Ontario shore. Stroking hard, we made for the donging sound of the green channel-marker bell, which still rocked in the aftereffects of the day before. Once past it, we were out in the shipping lanes where oceangoing freighters plied the waters. An early morning fog obscured the view to oncoming ships, so we listened instead for the booming engines. Even if the ships could see us, they could hardly be expected to slow down or maneuver around two tiny canoes.

Stokely Creek flows past one of Ontario's highest elevations, King Mountain. After a steep descent from the headwaters in Stokely Lake, the final meandering mile enters Lake Superior at Havilland Bay on the south side of Batchawana Bay.

The St. Mary's River, Lake Superior's only natural outflowing river, lies in the southeast corner of Whitefish Bay. The waters descend what remains of the rapids at Sault Ste. Marie and flow down to the lower Great Lakes. Before canals, locks, hydroelectric dams and industry stifled life in the river, whitefish were caught in great abundance. The mid-nineteenth-century author Anna Jameson wrote, "There is no more comparison between the whitefish of the lower lakes and the whitefish of St. Mary's, than between plaice and turbot, or between a clam and a Sandwich oyster. I have eaten tunny in the Gulf of Genoa, anchovies fresh out of the Bay of Naples and trout of the Salz-kammergut, and divers, other fish dainties rich and rare — but the exquisite, the refined white-fish, exceeds them all." In her book, *Winter Studies and Summer Rambles in Canada*, she recounts the traditions, ceremonies and stories from the lives of her Anishnabe friends at Sault Ste. Marie. I felt a kinship with the adventuresome spirit she portrayed. After running the Whitefish rapids, she was adopted into the Anishnabe family and honored with the name Wah–sàh–ge–wah–nó–quà, or "the woman of the bright foam."

She wrote eloquently about the native people dipping for whitefish: "I watched with a mixture of admiration and terror several little canoes which were fishing in the midst of the boiling surge, dancing and popping, about like corks. The canoe used for fishing is very small and light; one man (or woman more commonly) sits in the stern, and steers with a paddle; the fisher places himself upright on the prow, balancing a long pole with both hands, at the end of which is a scoop net. I never saw anything like these Natives. The manner in which they keep their position upon a footing of a few inches, is to me as incomprehensible as the beauty of their forms and attitudes, swayed by every movement and turn of their dancing, fragile barks, is so admirable."

Gusty southeasterly winds chased us north from where we had landed at Gros Cap two days earlier. Our golf umbrella served as a sail, pulling us along faster than we could paddle. We traveled like a train, Gary holding up the umbrella while I took hold of the rope tied to the stern of his canoe. After paddling and sailing in and out of rain squalls, we camped before nightfall on the Goulais Peninsula.

Two huge bites taken from the land on each side of the peninsula form the bays of Goulais and Batchawana. Batchawana means "bad inlet" and it refers to the narrows between Batchawana Island and the mainland where the current keeps the waters open all winter on an otherwise frozen bay. This bay is bounded on the north by headlands that dip gracefully one beyond the other, on the south by the Goulais Peninsula, on the west by the North and South Sandy Islands, and on the

Concentric rings of autumn color ripple out from the movements of a water strider.

east by the gray cliffs and old forested mountains of the Algoma Highlands. By late September, waterfowl of all kinds — loons, grebes, mergansers and pintails — would rendezvous here before heading east and south for the winter. Sandpipers, plovers, gulls, terns, horned larks, snow buntings and others would alight on the beaches of the Harmony, Chippewa and Batchawana Rivers to feed and rest before heading further south. Cradled in the arms of the bay is a large flat island. An eagle-eye perspective provided by the map showed it to be shaped like a large hot-air balloon complete with basket whisking westward toward the open lake. Scattered off to one side of the "basket," in the treetops of tiny islands called the Flowerpots, is a large blue-heron rookery.

The pale gray water surface, smooth as a satin sheet, was barely distinguishable from the equally colorless sky on the morning we paddled around Grindstone Point and into Batchawana Bay. Near the island, several loons were gliding over the silken waters. We moved in closer to eavesdrop on their rhythmic melodies of hoots and tremolos. In another three or four weeks, a hundred or more of their kind would leave inland nesting lakes and stage here before flying to coastal

When we canoed by the Flowerpots of Batchawana Bay, we spotted blue herons perched on the tree crowns.
We counted seventy large stick nests, indicating a long-used rookery.

Batchawana Bay is cradled in the arms of the Goulais Peninsula and the Algoma Highlands. Cliffs, beaches, rocky outcroppings and blazing sunsets are all part of kayaking on the bay.

waters for the winter. We hoped to be near Nipigon Bay by that time. Sighting the loons reminded us that Superior's temperamental autumn winds would soon be a concern. Already, in the third week of August, the days were shortening and sprigs of crimson were flaring up in the Highlands' vast sugar maple forests to the north and east.

The huge bays of Whitefish, Goulais and Batchawana were behind us. We had left the beautiful blond sands of Pancake Bay and the stony strand of Pancake Point that afternoon. Turning our canoes north, we cut V–shaped wakes through the unruffled waters of the open lake. From Hibbard Bay and Cozens Cove, we threaded the channel between black lava shoals and an indented, pockmarked shoreline so incredibly different from the softer, light–colored sandstone walls of the south shore.

Loons nest on Superior's shores in a few places, but more often they seek out quiet lakes inland. Nests are built right next to the water because a loon's legs are set too far back on its body to walk on land. Both the male and female raise the young, on average, two chicks per nest. A healthy lake with lots of live food such as minnows is necessary for the survival of the chicks. Every fall we count more than a hundred loons congregating together on Batchawana Bay before the fall migration.

In Mamainse Harbour, behind a protective barrier of islands, we passed several commercial fishing vessels tied at the dock. At the turn of the century, small fisheries like this one existed all around Lake Superior. Among some seventy different native fish species, the populations of whitefish, lake trout and herring were legendary. Long before the arrival of Europeans, native people were taking advantage of the places and seasons where great concentrations of fish appeared, such as the St. Mary's rapids. Reading many early European accounts, we have found references to the great quantities and sizes of fish caught. The fragility of the ecosystem was never understood until the large commercial fisheries systematically diminished fish populations to a minuscule proportion of their former numbers. For all its enormous size, Lake Superior does not contain much life in its cold, nutrient-deficient waters. Fish only appeared plentiful because of the high seasonal concentrations in very specific parts of the lake, at river mouths, in the shallows

The November storms of Lake Superior are legendary among Great Lakes mariners.
Near Mamainse Harbour, the treetops, normally 80 feet (24 m) above the lake surface, are whipped by the spray of the surging water.

and bays. During spawning runs and seasonal migrations, the fish were extremely vulnerable to the commercial fisheries and their mile-long nets. We trolled miles of Lake Superior, but our only meals came from the rivers.

To one particular ruby-throated hummingbird, our canoes must have looked like gigantic nectar-filled hibiscus blooms. It came darting out from the smooth boulder beach and over the clear waters of Alona Bay. Probing the length of each boat, the tiny bird appeared to be flying through a mist made by the blurring beat of its fairy wings. The iridescent red throat and green head glittered with jewel-like brilliance in the late afternoon light.

The extraordinary migration of the ruby-throated hummingbird would amaze any human traveler. It makes a round-trip between here and Central America, including a 500-mile (800 km), nonstop, twenty-four-hour flight over the open ocean of the Gulf of Mexico. We try to fathom the tenacity of life, to understand how something so small can survive the rigors of such a long journey. I thought of the Arctic terns we had once seen on Great Slave Lake, migrants that literally travel to the ends of the Earth between the North and South Poles each year. I thought of the bobolinks and the 6,000 miles (10,000 km) of flight between the Argentine pampas and Southern Ontario fields where we watch them each spring, and I felt humbled on our little voyage. But for now, we enjoyed a moment frozen in time. The misty whirring of the hummingbird's wings held the little body motionless over the red canoes, and the canoes themselves hung suspended on water as transparent as glass.

Water. Every day we contemplate the magical medium that we drink from, float on and swim in. The clear liquid coursing down valleys to fill Lake Superior is the very same substance from which seventy percent of our bodies are made. Above freezing, fish swim through it. Below freezing, it is powerful enough to crack a huge granite slab from the

Wistful clouds reflect the sun above Theano Point, Alona Bay.

The erratics in Alona Bay were scraped off the land by the glaciers and deposited here. Each one is unique in color, texture and pattern.

My canoe appeared as if it hung suspended in another dimension.
That this liquid carpet, pure and clear as air, could support my tiny craft, was to me as magical as flying.

face of a cliff. Mists, fogs and storm clouds are yet another of its mysterious forms that we lived with each day. And the beauty of Lake Superior, especially given the lake's great size, is that, for the most part, the water is clean and drinkable.

Water is always on the move, flowing through the soil, into the trunks of trees, up into the atmosphere and through our bodies. Just as the forests are deemed the lungs of our planet, so too, fresh water can be thought of as its blood. Within recent decades, Lake Superior's fur-bearing animals, fish and forests have been harvested indiscriminately. Any thought for the past and future of those species and their connection to the present has been hastily abandoned in the face of the profit promised by demand from faraway places. Lake Superior's water is no different. It is hard to imagine it flowing anywhere except down through the St. Mary's River. But, like the fish, the water may not be so infinite after all.

Feeding the agricultural heartland of the midwestern United States is a natural underground reservoir called the Ogallala Aquifer. Before it was tapped forty years ago, the aquifer contained about as

The tranquillity of solo canoe travel on the shores of Lake Superior.

Returning from Montreal Island before the storm.

much water as Lake Huron. It was thought to be constantly replenishing itself. However, in recent years, scientists have discovered that the level is dropping at a drastic rate. In another forty years, the reservoir could be dry. If it is possible to pump billions of gallons of oil across Alaska each day, it is hardly a wonder that eyes from the drying Midwest are turning eastward to gaze longingly on their nearest large water source, Lake Superior and the other Great Lakes.

Ruth Fletcher and Ward Conway built a cabin on the shores of Lake Superior at Montreal River Harbour. It is a small place built of locally cut jack-pine logs, heated by a woodstove, and lit with kerosene lamps and candles. Here, the term "running water" means Ward and the bucket brigade. Full of good spirit, this cabin has a large picture window with a view of the western horizon of the great lake. From this place, Ruth and Ward have enjoyed the comings and goings of storms, ice, wind, and a thousand different sunsets. Early one

Each rock is a unique face in a crowd of a hundred thousand speaking to us from a past too long ago to comprehend. Basalt, granite, gabbro, gneiss, quartz, all rolled here under the shroud of ice, then covered by meltwaters.

morning while we sat together, quietly sharing a pot of coffee and watching the morning unfold, Ruth starting laughing.

"Not long after we moved in here, a neighbor came by. He stepped inside the door and peered out the window. His first comment was, 'Nice place you have here but it's a shame there's nothing to look at.' "

"Nothing to look at!" I repeated incredulously, and we all started laughing.

"We have even seen things you shouldn't be able to see," Ward said. He explained that when the light conditions are right, the lighthouse signals from Caribou and Michipicoten Islands, both far beyond the horizon, can be seen.

Just south of the Montreal River below their cabin, we eased our canoes off smooth undulating folds of Shield rock that resembled the backs of whales, and slid them into the lake. It was a brilliant morning as we set off for Beaver Rock and Agawa Bay. The water was so clear that round rocks two canoe lengths below us looked close enough to touch. On

In all the months we have spent exploring Superior's shoreline, the only thing we can count on is her thrilling unpredictability and power. The variations on the simple theme of rock, sky, water and light are endlessly fascinating.

Beaver Rock, MacGregor Cove

one cobble beach, there was a group of large rocks, smooth and solid, like Henry Moore sculptures. Beneath them were nothing but black and white stones. I filled my pockets and ran my fingers through them again and again as I would a sack of marbles.

It was to be a day of special rocks. Water-smoothed black basalt resembling the flank of a killer whale at Laughing Brook. Sparkling grains of quartz in the beach below Beaver Rock. And Beaver Rock itself, two high hills of decreasing size ending in a low angled headland before the lake, resembling the silhouette of nature's industrious little dam-builder. Inscription Rock at Agawa Bay, where red ochre figures painted on the hundred-foot-high cliff connected us with the spirit of past humanity.

The people whose hands made the paintings were the same that held paddles shaped much like our own. They propelled their canoes over this same lake, bathed and drank from it, fished the streams, and surely marveled at the shape and color of the same rocks we had seen this day. They were people whose eyes saw storms approaching, whose ears heard thunder, whose noses caught the scent of damp earth, and whose taste buds relished blueberries. We could appreciate the physical aspect of their lives, yet the desires of our minds filled with vastly different stores of knowledge tore a rift between our worlds. Their survival depended upon their knowledge of the seasons, the animals and plants. In our world, digital watches and calendars keep track of the nebulous creature we call time. Paper and coins purchase food grown and raised in faraway places. I thought of the Anishnabe elder from Red Cliff who had held up two watches, one digital and one with hands. "Digital watches seem to be worn by

Near Steep Rock, black and white pebbles dapple the lake bottom like spots of sunshine and shade. When we scooped up handfuls of them and let them pour through our fingers, they felt like marbles. How interesting to fill one's pockets with some of the Earth's earliest history.

Dozens of red ochre paintings on the Agawa Rock wall have survived generations of rain, sun and ice to tell us much about the native way of life. Anishnabe shamans used this sacred rock canvas to depict travels, dreams, and the spirits. We were fortunate that our first view of the wall was from a canoe while on a long journey. Since then, we have returned in different seasons by the overland trail and along the frozen shore.

Truth is often a matter of perception and experience. As seen from the edge of the cliff, the figure skiing across the partly snow-covered bay could also be a figure sailing through shifting clouds between earth and space.

The tannic acid from cedars and other conifers growing along the riverbanks of the Sand River reacts with the pollen that settles on the surface. It foams up, forming a galaxy of swirling patterns.

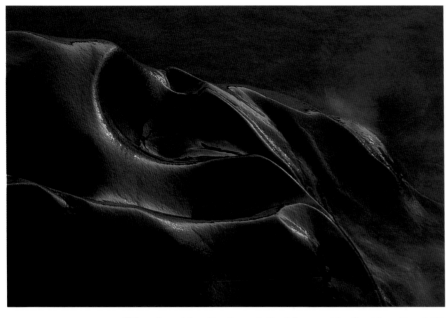

Where Laughing Brook meets the lake, a patch of wet basalt rock lit by the reflection of the setting sun resembles smooth whale skin.

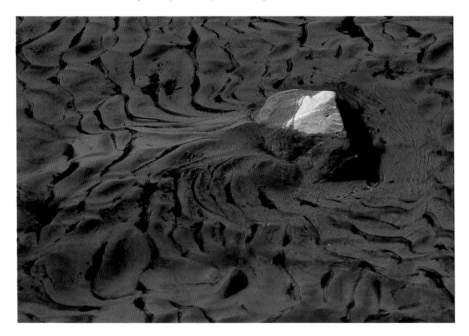

A stream flowing over brown-sugar sand at Agawa Bay.

everyone today. They only show the present time," he explained, "but on the one with hands, you can see history and future." Out here on the lake, our days were measured in paddle strokes and the time it took for the sun to cross the sky. Our journey's progress was scheduled by the weather. There was a comforting reassurance in the rhythms of the land, for which there is no equivalent substitute in human society. The recurring cycles of the seasons are more than merely entertaining phenomena; they remind us of our connection to the eternal rhythms of the universe.

For the past hour we had been paddling along, remembering our discoveries of old trappers' cabins made during both winter ski and summer canoe trips. These simple structures, fours walls and a roof of weathered hand–peeled logs chinked with moss, were often still furnished with a woodstove, table, chair, shelves and a bunk. Mice and squirrel droppings would always be liberally sprinkled over everything. Sometimes we would even surprise a porcupine busy inside gnawing away at a cupboard or other human salted delicacies. We recalled the feeling that the past occupant's spirit still lingered close by. A short while later we arrived in a pretty little cove where a curving sand beach looked too inviting to pass by. While I was swimming, Gary went exploring and found an old cabin set back from the beach. Poplars screened the view to the lake. The door was ajar, so he pushed it open and walked inside to find the usual. A mischievous thought prompted him to lay on the bunk. Mean–while, I was following Gary's tracks down the beach. I, too, found the cabin and the door cracked open. Just as my eyes grew accustomed to the darkness, I saw a body lying on the lower bunk. My heartbeat stepped up double time as I backed out the door, a scream caught in my throat. Then, from inside, I heard Gary's muffled laughter.

In Agawa Bay, patches of snow and ice like miniature glaciers
blanket the north-facing slopes along Superior's shores well into the month of May.

The Sand, or Pinguisibi, River flows through the interior of Lake Superior Provincial Park, beginning at the headwaters on Sand Lake at Mile 138 on the Algoma Central Railway.

On the Sand River, as on many of the north shore rivers, there are swift rapids and falls in the final mile above Lake Superior.

The islands, bays and beaches near Gargantua Harbour.

Between the Baldhead River and Old Woman Bay, an elbow of land juts into Lake Superior. The islands and bays are part of the bewitching shoreline of Gargantua. Part of the east side of Gargantua Island forms a natural harbor with a high lichen-covered wall. Curving out from the base of this cliff is a small cobble beach where we left our canoes while we explored what was left of another Lake Superior lighthouse. A steep stairway beside the wall brought us to the highest point on the island, where the original lighthouse once stood. Nothing much remains of it except the crumbled foundations. Back down on the cobble beach, we searched for the lighthouse keeper's living quarters, which we eventually found back in the forest, nestled some distance from the lake. While inside the cabin, we imagined ourselves to be the assistant keeper and his daughter caught in the November storm of 1940. High winds and waves destroyed the light on the tip of the island. And despite the house's protected position, the wind caught the spray and hurled it against the cabin door all night long. By morning, the cabin was encased in ice and the assistant keeper and his daughter were imprisoned behind the icebound walls until friends from the mainland arrived with axes to chop them free.

As we paddled north from Gargantua Island, the shroud of fog slowly lifted, revealing a prehistoric landscape. The humped-up shapes of black volcanic islands rising from Superior became the backs of marine dinosaurs in the steaming tropics of long-ago saltwater seas. I almost expected to hear the explosive sound of whales breaching. Our course between the islands took us beneath a sheer cliff on the largest island, mottled orange, gray and green with a profusion of lichens. From the water, gnarled cedars hung down, partially concealing the entrance to a cave. Above it, there was another black void and, still higher, a large white-washed nest.

A black bear cub searches for its mother and sibling. We accidentally disturbed them while rounding a point with the wind in our faces.

Beating on a skin drum tightened with the fire's warmth generates a deep, primordial heartbeat that echoes around the walls of the secret cave and out into the night.

We landed soundlessly along the margin between lake and land, tiptoeing along the beautiful rocks where yarrow and saxifrage had taken root. Up through the lush forest, our footfalls were silenced by the spongy bed of verdant mosses. More like an amphitheater with its high ceiling and walls scooped up like a bowl, the cave was enchanting and haunting. On one side of the cave there are ledges in the crumbling, dark red rock where people once collected the hematite for making red ochre to paint on the walls at Agawa.

Just after we pushed off from shore with our canoes parallel to the island and facing south, I heard Gary's voice in hushed urgency whisper to me to look up on the cliff. A shaft of sunlight that had just broken through the clouds streamed down between the V-gap of two pinnacles on the cliff, clipping off the lip of a lower crag. A peregrine falcon perched there in perfect silhouette. Seconds later our canoes had drifted past the only clear view to the sky and the backlit form of the large falcon. The dark gray of its body melded with the color of the cliff, leaving only a raptor's yellow talons and black facial mask easily visible. A moment later the peregrine took flight, crossed the mouth of the cave, banked and, appearing to fly right into the cliff, it disappeared.

In a wonderful place at the mouth of the Gargantua River, we set up our tent and went for a walk down the length of the beach. Sixty years ago, when Gargantua's lumbering and fishing activities supported several families year-round and many more during the summer, numerous canoeists and fishermen made forays into this protected bay and camped here. At the western end of the beach, a narrow channel separated an island from the mainland. Since the water was only knee-deep, we were able to follow its sinuous curves on foot. As the bay widened out, ripples originating from the shadowed shores caught our attention. We pressed in beneath the trees before moving around the point. A dimpled pattern across the sandy lake-bottom led to the far end of the bay where a moose was feeding on underwater plants. For a time we played a game of freezing motionless when her head came up, and then sneaking forward a few more steps as soon as it ducked beneath the surface. It was only when she lifted her head for the final time, giving a full body shake and throwing off a rainbow halo of spray, that we noticed how long our feet and legs had been submerged. They were completely numb. Then the cow moose stepped off toward the tip of another island, where we suddenly noticed what looked like four table-legs stuck in the sand behind a beaver-felled birch. A moose calf pranced into the opening, across the narrows, and up into the forest behind its mother.

We were not alone among the islands off the Gargantua peninsula. Out of the porous rock, faces emerge by the dozens, their peaceful expressions providing an ever-changing audience. Surrounding them were strange black promontories, the gargoyles of Gargantua, and beaches of intriguing red, black and white pebbles with agates mixed in. The soft contours of surrounding hills framed the scene. It was easy to feel the power of this place that held such spiritual significance for the Anishnabe. Missionaries intent on preaching their beliefs renamed Nanabijou's Chair "Devil's Chair" and they called the island with caves that held red ochre and birchbark scrolls "Devil's Warehouse Island." Instead of trying to understand the power that such places gave the Anishnabe, the missionaries instilled a sense of fear. Their religion turned people against the places that had meant so much in their lives.

On our map, I marked Nanabijou's Chair, the Anishnabe name for the throne-shaped rock that rose before us now. The Chair faces east and, on this bright morning, it was filled with sunshine. Dotted here and there, hardy purple bellflowers were anchored in the cracks. It was warm on the dark rock where I sat and sketched for a while. A cool northwest breeze flowed through an arched doorway and window in the back of the Chair where I had a view to the elongated reefs and the great lake reaching out to Michipicoten Island 15 miles (25 km) away. Having grown up on the books of C. S. Lewis, especially *The Lion, the Witch and the Wardrobe*, I was fascinated with the idea of my own Narnias. To go between other worlds was normal on Superior, whether we were meandering from a fogbound lakeshore to a warm oasis behind a screen of islands, or stepping through the hole in the Chair, going instantly from a sunny, protected place to a cold and windy world hidden from the sun.

We left more tobacco, a personal touchstone with the land. For a moment, your life feels immediate. You are aware that you are the breath that flows in and out of your lungs and the water that passes beneath your canoe. Like the wave that rises with separate character from the lake yet is the lake, I feel that I, too, am all that exists. Leaving tobacco marks time to allow our senses to draw in the story a place reveals to us. Smell the rock, breathe the air, taste the water, hear the myriad of songs on the land. Everything has a song. You never forget such places, ever.

Pieces of planking, beams with square nails, steel sheathing and other shipwreck flotsam that we found strewn along the inhospitable shoreline of Bushy Bay showed us that one or more ships had foundered here in fairly recent history. Enough was left to encourage discovery of more parts to the story. With the lake lying unruffled beneath a blanket of fog, it was an ideal morning for sleuthing around. We groped our way in and out of bays, past the cliffs and into Old Woman Bay. The cold, damp day only added to our imagined picture of the bleakness faced by any survivors from these wrecks. We turned several times to look at the immense black cliffs that towered over the lake. Finally the fog lifted momentarily, revealing more than the black wall. The humor in the strong oblong face

Lake Superior's terraced beaches mark old shorelines. Although the changes are imperceptible to us, the land is still rebounding from the weight of glacial ice. Such knowledge is of great interest to us on our travels, as we try to imagine what life has been like along these shores for the past 10,000 years.

Poplar trees sprout buds in the lengthening days of spring.

with one winking eye caught us quite by surprise. Simultaneously we both burst out, "There she is, the Old Woman!" Elated, we winked back, then turned and paddled off to Michipicoten Harbour.

From Vincenzo Coronelli's map of 1688 to Jacques Nicolas Bellin's *Lac Superieur* of 1755, Michipicoten River is common to all, tucked into the northeast corner of the lake. Ever since our first canoe trip together down the Missinaibi River to James Bay in 1980, Gary and I had thought about following the entire historic route from Lake Superior via the Michipicoten River. Long known to travelers before the white man's arrival, the Michipicoten–Missinaibi route provided the easiest and shortest link between Superior and salt water. The Hudson's Bay Company took advantage of this route, establishing a fur-

Descending the second-last drop of the Magpie River before it joins with the Michipicoten and flows into Lake Superior.

trading post here that remained in existence fifteen years longer than either Grand Portage or Fort William. But now there is little left except the old grave site high up on the north bank overlooking the island, where the Hudson's Bay regional headquarters once stood.

Carving out its serpentine curves in the glacial debris, the Michipicoten finds its way out to the lake through a narrow throat. Framing both sides of the river mouth are beautiful beaches. We chose the terraced beach to the south for our camp. A path behind our campsite led to a high sandy bank of the Michipicoten River. We had a grand view of the river winding out toward the setting sun where, in silhouette upon the bay, numerous boats trolled back and forth, fishing for salmon.

Snow clouds over Michipicoten Harbour Lighthouse, Michipicoten Bay.

By candlelight inside the tent, I leafed through the copied historical maps I had made in the map library months ago. Both John Cary's 1807 map and Jacques Nicolas Bellin's 1755 map marked the Philippeaux Islands north of the Keweenaw. Bellin's map also showed a huge island southwest of Michipicoten Bay named Isle Pontchartrain. Neither are found on any modern map. I recalled a day that we had spent on the south shore weaving through the ribbon of reefs below the Porcupine Mountains, where strange fogs and layered hot and cold air created mirage islands, perhaps explaining Bellin's stories of his travels along the south shore.

"Twenty miles further to the north, glistened the broad expanse of the great lake at the entrance of the bay (Keweenaw). There lay a tall, bluish island, with which the mirage played in an infinity of ways during our voyage. At times the island rose in the air to a spectral height then sank again and faded away, while at another moment we saw the islands hovering over one another into the air."

Ahead of us and west along the coast lay another island marked on all the maps, from Dablon's 1673 *Fens des Terres* to our own 1973 topographic edition. Unlike Pontchartrain, it was not conjured from refracting light and reflections, but by all accounts its haunted coast seems to exist somewhere between both worlds. The home of giants and gods, precious metals and exquisite stones, Michipicoten was long thought to be a floating island. All the way from Whitefish Bay, islands such as Parisienne, Montreal and the Lizards had the same quality of appearing sometimes near, sometimes far, sometimes invisible behind the fog or, in one strange instance, mirrored upside down upon the sky. Lured by copper, indigenous miners of the Old Copper Culture were drawn to Michipicoten Island in the same way they were drawn to Isle Royale, the Keweenaw and Mamainse Harbour thousands of years ago. Hunters in every century made the crossing in pursuit of waterfowl and game abundant on Michipicoten's inland lakes. Then, much later, came the era of ships and wrecks and the families who manned the lighthouses. All these curiosities were tumbling around in my mind as I imagined us setting off on the 11-mile (18 km) traverse from Point Isacor on the mainland to Michipicoten Island. Words melted into an indecipherable scrawl as the pen, logbook and map slipped from my hands. Gary leaned over, giving me a hug and kiss, and blowing out the candle. "Happy dreams."

The waving figure appears to be a tiny spirit emerging from the fog surrounding the spectacular Denison Falls on the Dog River. This falls was the last portage on a trip from the headwaters to Lake Superior.

THE JOURNEY WEST

Michipicoten River to Kama Bay

Early September

FROM THE FRESH COATS OF RED AND WHITE PAINT ON THE BUILDINGS, WALKWAYS AND DOCKS AT THE Michipicoten Lighthouse, it was obvious that the lighthouse keeper was in residence. Gary noticed him first, a tiny figure balancing on a ladder with a paint can in one hand and paintbrush in the other, working his way across the front of the keeper's living quarters. We waved. The man practically leapt to the ground without touching a step and ran to the dock to greet us. A beaming and breathless Dave Waddell introduced himself as the lighthouse keeper and eagerly invited us in for tea. An early September gale had kept us in Michipicoten Harbour for three days, and even though we had made the best of it by washing our clothes and picking up supplies, we wanted to take advantage of the fair weather today. So, he chatted from shore about the weather, the spectacular shoreline ahead of us, and of lighthouse life. "One of my favorite photographs was taken on someone's wedding day in Michipicoten Harbour," he said. "All the lighthouse keepers came in from the lake in their boats no bigger than mine." He nodded toward his own small boat pulled up on shore. "In the picture, their boats are lined up along the beach so you can read the sterns and one says Caribou Island."

"That's fifty miles from shore, opposite Montreal River Harbour!" I exclaimed. He nodded. We knew the island from the map, further from shore than any other on the lake. Superior's counterclockwise currents actually circle around it.

"Wouldn't catch me out there," Dave said emphatically, "although I would like a chance to see more of the shore where you're going. Maybe some day when I'm not manning the light. I'm not complaining, though. I'm here seven months of the year and I love it."

We told him we hoped to be back soon and then we picked up our paddles and moved off around the headland.

Weaving in and out of the natural harbors, past creeks and large rivers, we traveled tirelessly all day, aware that we were embarking on the longest section of wilderness shoreline on Lake Superior. One hundred and ten miles (175 km) lay between us and our next port of call, the Pukaskwa National Park headquarters at Hattie Cove. Near the Dog River, families of mergansers patrolled the shallows with military precision. Catching them unawares was always fun because we could see them darting off in all directions pursuing minnows in the clear waters. An osprey circled overhead and then dove suddenly. Missing the catch, it plunged again, this time grasping what looked like a rainbow trout. Beating the air heavily with long angular wings, this white-headed fishing eagle swept across the surface then rose into the uppermost branches of a spruce tree, the fish firmly clutched in its talons.

We rode our solo whitewater canoes like spirited horses through the Dog River's dark gorges.

Further west, where the land grew steep with great lumpy ridges, we paddled swiftly to the safety beyond the Eagle River cliffs and Point Isacor, and stopped for a break in a shallow lagoon. Two bright-eyed and bewhiskered faces appeared above the surface like a couple of swiveling periscopes. Diving playfully, the otters resurfaced a bit closer. One snorted and the other snuffled, giving the impression they were conversing about the strange creatures that had suddenly appeared in their midst.

Northwest of the Pukaskwa River, we glided into a beautiful deep bay named Imogene Cove on our topographic map. More appropriately it could have been named Pukaskwa Cove for the Anishnabe family that once lived in the area. For twelve years, from 1918 to 1930, the Lake Superior Paper Company logged pulpwood on the Pukaskwa River. The company's winter logging camp, known as the Depot, was situated at the back of Imogene Cove. We came ashore on the wide, sandy beach. I rifled through the contents of my logbook to find a sketch of the Depot drawn for us by Ruth Fletcher's Uncle Lee at Montreal River Harbour. The drawing was like a map, enabling us to piece together a picture of the Depot whose history is now overgrown by a wild tangle of saplings and wildflowers.

At False Dog Harbour, deep scratches, or striations, were scraped out by the glacial ice as it dragged loose materials across the hard bedrock surface.

A week-long whitewater canoe trip on the Pukaskwa River is followed by 60 miles (100 km) of flatwater canoeing along the wonderfully isolated shoreline to reach the community of Michipicoten Harbour.

In mid-June the spring flood was already subsiding on the Pukaskwa River, making it possible for us to run sections of Ringham's Gorge.

We followed the bay around to the spring. On one side there had been a bunkhouse, cookery and three stables. Further in from the lake, a hay shed was used from December to May. The barn boss's shack, behind all this, was home to the man who fed and cared for the thirty teams of horses. Other buildings were identified as the one-legged harness maker's cabin, the doctor's office, the black-smith, the scaler's cabin, the warehouse, office and house. The only structure still standing was the Fletcher cabin, where Lee spent his childhood, but by the looks of the sagging roof meeting the tall grasses, this cabin, too, was being reclaimed by the earth.

We crossed the creek past the place where another bunkhouse and cookery had existed along with the six-holer outhouse. According to Lee's map, there had also been a root cellar and a pigpen. The graveyard was overgrown with a profusion of daisies and wild roses. One of the several unmarked fenced graves contained a wooden monument adorned with an elaborate cross of metal hearts.

The cobble beaches along the eastern side of Lake Superior are littered with pulp logs, escapees from the once huge rafts of logs that were pulled across the lake from such places as the Depot. These rafts contained the winter's cut of five to six thousand cords. Three large tugboats maneuvered the ponderous rafts to the paper mill in Sault Ste. Marie. A great hazard for the slow-moving procession were the storms that broke up the rafts and scattered logs for miles up and down the shoreline. In every bay and along every cobble beach, we found reminders of the logging days. Bolts and rings embedded in the bedrock, old boom logs with rusty lengths of chain still fastened to the holes in each end, and the pulpwood itself worn and pounded from years of tumbling against rocky shores.

The Pukaskwa river mouth marks the southeastern boundary to Pukaskwa National Park. A short distance upstream, we discovered the place where the river makes a final spectacular plunge through the tortured gray rock of Schist Falls

Sunset at the mouth of the Pukaskwa River.

The cobble beach at Cascade Falls is one of the most picturesque campsites on the entire Lake Superior shoreline.

before spilling out into Superior. In the pools below, we cast out our lines. Gary's line went taut first and a shimmering silver form broke the surface. Gary had a lively fight before he reeled the fish to the side of the canoe. He reached over, grabbing the lure with the pliers. With a quick flick, the barbless hook slipped free. A flash of a pink stripe along the trout's flank told us there were rainbows here. We trolled around the bay and caught three more, the last of which we kept for dinner.

There is a fine lighthouse on Otter Island, complete with a large two-story lighthouse-keeper's house tucked in the protected bay facing the mainland. Off the end of the light-house dock, in water too deep and cold to retrieve, we saw an old bathtub. The sight was made even more incongruous because we knew it was the very one Ruth Fletcher's grandmother had ordered from the Eaton's catalog when she lived at the Depot. After surviving the trip on the paper company tugboat, the bathtub was carried up to the Fletcher cabin and placed near the woodstove. Some time later it was transported to the Otter Island lighthouse dock where it served as a planter for flowers and then, finally, ended up in the lake.

We followed the trail leading from the house to the light high on the exposed northwestern tip of the island. From there we had a panoramic view from Michipicoten Island all the way to the Pukaskwa coast. I realized how differently I now viewed the vastness of the horizon that lay between the two. Instead of just water, I could see in my mind's eye what was beyond. Suddenly, the feeling of being connected to the entire lake was no longer an abstract thought. It was real. We had canoed there.

That night we set up our tent on the beach below Cascade Falls, one of the most picturesque campsites on the whole Superior shoreline.

Fine mist along the 40-mile (60 km) Pukaskwa Hiking Trail shrouds the view to the final drop on the White River.

A heaving swell shattered the thin ice into a million fragments.
Wind and wave heap the pulverized chips into windthrows for miles along the shore.

The White River

For the next two days and three nights, we were windbound. It could not have happened in a more perfect place. Both mornings we showered beneath the icy waters tumbling over the last ledge of the Cascade River. Then we went hiking. The first day it rained so hard that we hugged the coast, rounding as many points of land as possible before turning back late in the afternoon. On the second day, wind-whipped clouds scudded across the burning blue sky. The Cascade beckoned us inland along its wild corridor flowing down from the Pukaskwa interior. We departed from camp soon after breakfast, taking cameras, binoculars, and daypacks with extra clothing and food. From the back of the beach, it was a short climb up through gnarly cedars and balsams to reach the top of the first waterfalls. From the lip of the falls, we looked down on the beach. Monstrous green waves rolling in along the stony shore made our tent and two red canoes look awfully insignificant.

Lake-tumbled smooth rocks made us think of bowling balls. When tossed, one of these rocks would bounce a dozen times before settling again.

We made our way through short boulder–strewn canyons of steep walls and dark pools with waterfall after waterfall. We scrambled up boulders, down crevasses and along ledges, gripping with our fingers and toes. Everywhere the land had been scoured, gouged, broken and molded. Further in from the lake, the river broadened into a series of looping curves. The gravel bars were dimpled with fresh moose and timber wolf tracks. A flock of sandhill cranes took flight when we appeared around one river bend.

I fished the deep, shaded pools for speckled trout while Gary photographed patterns in the water and sand. In the late afternoon, we turned back, arriving at the top of the falls just in time to see the sun melt into the lake. Overhead, like sails on fire, the ragged clouds swept across the darkening ocean of sky.

That night, the mesmerizing dance of light in the glowing embers of the fire was reflected in the heavenly theatrics of the aurora borealis. It was as if we were in a great glass dome over which someone was pouring milk. Enormous shafts of light pulsed upward, sharp strong fingers glinting green above the horizon. Land and sky surged with the fluidity and power of the Waussnodae. In winter, the Anishnabe interpreted the northern lights as the fires burning in the lodges of their ancestors. In other seasons, they were attributed to the illumin-ated path provided for the souls to find their way to the Land of Peace.

At the base of a broad, terraced cobble beach, we lifted the bows of our fully loaded canoes onto a small log. Using it as a roller on the bed of rounded rocks, we hauled the boats beyond the pawing grasp of the swell. Walking away from the canoes, we noticed how the rocks that embraced the bay in a high unbroken arch were neatly arranged,

These bony-fingered rocks are constantly bathed in the polluted waters that flow from Marathon's pulp and paper mill. Individual citizens, environmental groups, schools and organizations have banded together throughout the Lake Superior Basin to protect these waters from toxic contamination.

Pic Island at sunset.

By mid-September, blueberry leaves burn scarlet along a ridge overlooking the islands in Mink Harbour, east of the Coldwell Peninsula.

---

increasing to the size of bowling balls. Half a dozen canoe-lengths above us, the storm line marked the highest reach of the waves with an array of debris. Among the driftwood and pulp logs were ship's timbers, bits of heavy rope, smashed wooden crates and fishing net floats. Above this line, the beach was less sloped, the rocks sharp-edged and rough with crisp curls of lichen.

If there is one plant that comes to mind along the Pukaskwa shoreline, it is the lichens. Unlike the harebells waving their purple faces from the cracks and crevasses near shore, these pioneer plants often appear to be part of a tree or a rock rather than an entity unto themselves. Course gray tufts of a lichen called old-man's beard adorn the spruce and balsam trees. Brittle star patterns splash over the bare rocks like spilled orange paint. Goblet and red-topped soldier lichens march down among the wintergreen and mosses. A relationship between fungus and algae thousands of years old has developed these tough little plants that range

Camped on the Coldwell Peninsula opposite Pic Island. At daybreak that morning, a cow and bull moose wandered down the creek to pay us a visit.

over an area covering a tenth of the Earth's surface and half the boreal forest we were now in. They provide nesting material for several dozen species of birds and food for countless small creatures such as northern flying squirrels, as well for caribou and other large animals, especially in harsh weather. Anishnabe people gathered them for medicine and dyes.

High above the lake on this old cobble beach, lichens dappled the strange depressions known as Pukaskwa pits. Long ago, human hands removed the rocks, leaving small and large pits. The intended uses and purposes remain somewhat of a mystery, although it seems clear that there were several. One afternoon Gary was crouched inside a pit. While pressing his ear to the rocks, hoping that somehow they would whisper their story to him, the clatter of my footfall telegraphed through to him instead. At that moment, he imagined himself a hunter and the clatter to be caribou hooves on the cobble beach. It seemed highly likely that a hunter could have used a pit as a blind from which to ambush caribou when they wandered close by. It also seemed possible that large pits could have been temporary shelters for a family or a place to

The Group of Seven artist Lawren Harris immortalized these undulating curves in a painting simply titled Pic Island.
He made the original sketches not far from our campsite on the Coldwell Peninsula.

cache food. All the small pits we found in exposed places had one thing in common: a view to an island offshore. Perhaps they were spiritual places where fasting and physical exposure encouraged vision quests, dreams where animal spirits promised guidance and meaning to life. In these small pits, young Anishnabe may have marked their initiation to adulthood with spiritual journeys.

Our breath condensed in little white puffs between us and the roof of the tent, yet another promise of fall. Yesterday a flock of Canada geese numbering in the hundreds passed over in a long, wavering V. Eager to greet the first rays of sun shooting through the spruce spires, we were on the water in less than an hour. The scene was rocky knolls and sheer cliffs. When it was calm, we could paddle in close enough to touch the rock walls by the shore. Spidery arms of quartz shot through pink and gray granite. Staircases of basalt known as diabase dikes run down from the forest edge and disappear into the dark depths of the lake like wide black ribbons.

Even when the surface is barely moving, the lake's presence is still immense and powerful. Heading north from the Swallow River, there were 40 miles (60 km) of shoreline indented with protected coves, carved with river valleys and speckled with islands. In the canoes, we traveled quietly through the lives of many birds and animals. A great blue heron stalked the shallows. A trio of otters dove playfully around the canoes. Mink skittered along the shore. A mother bear and her two cubs paid us little mind. We were within a stone's throw before they bounded off.

From one natural harbor to the next, we rounded headlands. These were often tricky places where bouncy cross-current swells reverberated off the shore. Wind and waves played other tricks, sometimes creating white-knuckle, paddle-clenching experiences. Approaching Oiseau Bay was one such time. We had been gleefully surfing the long, oily-smooth swells when one of the waves crested beneath our canoes. The instability unnerved us. Cresting wave followed cresting wave and, in moments, we were suddenly aware of how unsafe we felt. Ordinarily, the distance from shore would have felt small, but the icy spray numbing our hands was a grim reminder of what a capsize would mean. It was with a deep and thankful sigh that we rounded Oiseau Point into island-studded Oiseau Bay.

The tracks of wolf, mice and weasels crisscrossed the beach, and overlapping them all were the fresh, fat, pigeon-toed paw prints of black bear. We followed them to the mouth of Oiseau Creek, where upright living trees protruded from a sandy delta, giving the appearance of a pond without water. These flats were covered with the webbed tracks of Canada geese. The entire mouth of the river had altered course when a sudden, devastating flood, caused by the collapse of a beaver dam, carved out the clay and sandstone banks upstream.

A mile offshore in Ashburton Bay, the naked, glacial-scarred shoals known as Fitzsimmons Rocks
offered us a brief respite from September headwinds.

Two days later we paddled through the islands off the Coldwell Peninsula. An afternoon wind forced us to land on small Fitzsimmons Rocks in the middle of Ashburton Bay. There we sat until dark waiting for the wind to die.

Pic Island was behind us and Bottle Point somewhere ahead. That was all I knew. It had been my idea to wait on Fitzsimmons Rocks until the wind died, and then cover some miles by moonlight. But heavy clouds rolled in, leaving us in pitch darkness. We couldn't even see one another. Only the feel of an offshore wind and the toss of rebounding surf against rock kept us going in one direction. The swell lifting and lowering our canoes felt huge. I braced for the impact of breaking waves, but they were always much less forceful than the ones I imagined. I directed my flashlight toward shore, but I couldn't see land. It was an eerie yet thrilling sensation and I knew Gary was enjoying it as much as I was.

After half a night of paddling, we finally groped our way into shore and made camp. At first light we had a view to the Slate Islands, lying 8 miles (13 km) off the shores of Terrace Bay. These were a group of islands we had long been looking forward to visiting. In a mother-of-pearl sky, small puffs of cumulus clouds floated into view like smoke from a distant campfire. I thought, as the bows of our canoes sliced through the satiny waters like knives through ribbon, that we could not have a more suitable day. We had taken the precaution of fastening our spray tarps and lowering the seats to the most stable position for the long crossing.

"I was just thinking of the distance to the islands tipped up on end," Gary said. I nodded as we both pondered the three-dimensional worlds of fish and birds.

As we drew closer, the black cliffs metamorphosed into contorted shapes of strange unearthly beings. We would not have expected otherwise, for tens of millions of years ago, a meteorite hurtled in from space, colliding with the Earth at this place. Erosion and weathering has dispersed much of the original meteorite through the basin. A geologist had shown us a large-scale geological survey map of this circular archipelago of islands. The chaotic conglomerate stippled with bits of silver and gold and marbled with a bewildering array of elements and minerals forms a highly challenging jigsaw.

With entrances to the circle on the east and west sides, the Slate Islands provide sanctuary from the openness of the lake. We passed by Barnard Point between Mortimer and Patterson Islands. In some of the bays, we could look 40 feet (12 m) down into the clear waters where piles of pulpwood logs litter the bottom. Patterson, largest of the islands, has a heavily indented shoreline. Its interior is dotted with lakes, high ridges, and a magnetic anomaly that made our compass go crazy. Hiking across the center of the island was like hiking across an open park with an almost complete lack of ground cover. The

In December, frigid temperatures sweep across the lake, drawing warmth from the waters
until they stiffen and clasp the islands of Terrace Bay in icy talons.

overgrazed island is populated by the descendants of an ancient north shore caribou herd.

On the water at dusk, we heard a branch snap near shore. Edging in close to the point, we rounded it in time to see a caribou step into the lake. Breathless and paddling as hard as we could, it was all we could do to catch up to this tireless swimmer. All I could see of it was the antler-adorned head tilted back and a short curved tail. When it reached the far shore, the caribou's legs never missed a beat. One moment the large splayed hooves were pulling water, and the next, they were touching land. Water streamed from its thick coat as it emerged. The smooth, effortless transition from water to land made it look as if the lake was giving birth to the animal. With a stiff-legged gait, it trotted off down the cobbles and disappeared up a well-worn path.

Before logging and settlement along the north shore, nomadic woodland caribou roamed over a wide area in small family groups. Their winter diet consisted of reindeer lichen and old-man's beard that grew in mature boreal forests of balsam fir, spruce and jack pine. In summer, the caribou browse on different types of deciduous plants such as thimbleberries. Second-growth forests followed the loggers, and the more readily adaptable moose moved in along with human settlement. The caribou were easy prey for the human hunters. Declining habitat, combined with heavy hunting pressure, further reduced their population. Along the north shore, the caribou are now only found in isolated pockets such as in the Slate Islands.

In the first half of this century, timber companies logged the north shore's boreal forest for pulpwood and paper. The trees, cut in early winter, were floated down the rivers in spring and collected in bays by huge free-floating booms. A woody carpet on the lake bottom, boom logs, anchors drilled in rock, and pulp logs scattered along the north shore beaches are the remains of the days when logs were towed to mills in Sault Ste. Marie and Thunder Bay.

On a wonderfully calm afternoon, we scrambled to the top of an outcropping of columnar basalt
along the southern shore of Simpson Island to look for any hint of approaching winds on the horizon .

After almost eighty days on the lake, we still looked forward with undiminished enthusiasm to cooking our evening meal over an open fire. Made from several sticks of driftwood that quickly turned to glowing coals, the fire would, by morning, be nothing more than fine ash. With a pot of coffee between us, we leaned against a weather-worn and bone-white cedar log. It was a time to collect our thoughts and close the day, as if to break up the long, unending sentence of the journey. Overhead, a hundred billion stars shone through the fabric of atmosphere until we had a clear view of the untouchable, timeless heavens.

Gesturing northward with the flashlight beam, I outlined the Big Dipper. From there I traced a straight line from the two outside stars on the Big Dipper's ladle to locate the North Star, which shines off the tip of the Little Dipper's handle. Draco, the dragon, winds around the Little Dipper, its head a box shape near little cone-headed Cepheus. Off to the side lies Andromeda, reaching out to touch Pegasus's wing, and nearby is her mother, W-shaped Cassiopeia. Stargazers of long ago recognized recurring patterns, understood the families of stars, and passed on their own explanations. An Anishnabe story tells how summer and winter came to be. In it, the Big Dipper is part of the Fisher, not the Bear as we usually know it. The Fisher is persuaded by his son to bring warm weather to the Earth where it was always so cold. Together, Fisher and his larger cousin, the Wolverine, manage to jump into skyland where they free all the birds and open a hole in the sky for the warm weather to reach the Earth. The sky people chased them away, but only after they opened a hole big enough to allow warm weather in for half the year. Wolverine escaped back to Earth, but Fisher was shot with an arrow by the sky people. His great sacrifice was rewarded by Gitchee Manitou, who placed him in the sky. In the spring, Fisher stands on his feet, but come autumn, he rolls over on his back again.

For many of the Earth's inhabitants, from sailors on the open ocean to the little yellow-rumped warblers that we frequently saw hopping along the rocks next to shore, the North Star and surrounding constellations have long been reliable navigation aids. With our binoculars, we could see the brilliant colors of the planets and stars much better than with our naked eyes. And every now and then one of us would glimpse a spear of light streaking across the heavens. If I could ride a falling star, what would I see of planet Earth? A blue and white pearl suspended in the great black velvet void of mystery, the same mystery that permeates every moment of every day in every scrap of life. The twinkling reflections of stars on the water mirrored infinity. It was once thought that infinity lived here on Earth too, infinite animals, infinite birds, infinite space for human beings to live.

For the better part of two days, damp mists crept in from the east, hanging low and heavy with a sense of foreboding. The long summer days were over. Birches tinged with yellow were beginning to color the rising hills. The lack of birdsong and the increased winds foretold the season's change. Traversing Schreiber Channel, we made for Copper Island, the beginning of an island chain that stretches all the way to Thunder Bay. Whorls of black water were swept back behind us on each stroke as we neared McGarvey's Shoal, chartering a course similar to the ill-fated voyage of a luxury steam schooner in 1911. Almost 300 feet (100 m) below us, resting peacefully in her cold tomb, lies the *Gunilda*.

The *Gunilda* was built in a Scottish shipyard and then sailed across the Atlantic to the United States. Her second summer's voyage to Lake Superior was undertaken late in the season by her owner, the oil millionaire W. L. Harkness. When the *Gunilda* docked in at the fishing hamlets of Port Coldwell and Jackfish, the local people had never in their lives seen anything like the grandeur of this ship and its crew. Despite his wealth, Harkness thought it an extravagance to hire a fisherman to pilot them through the islands and so the *Gunilda* met its untimely end, piling up on McGarvey's Shoal just off Copper Island. All aboard survived unscathed, but during the salvage operation, the *Gunilda* filled with water and sank in deep waters just off the reef, much to Harkness's despair. Rumors of lost treasure lured divers for years afterward, some even to their death. But a further tragedy is the *Gunilda* herself. The lake claimed the ship whole. Far below the ravages of storm and waves, the cold waters have preserved her beautifully. All the damage she has since sustained has been from grappling hooks and anchors, human scavengers picking at her bones like vultures. The talk of bringing the whole ship to the surface is sadly still alive. Cradled in scaffolding, the *Gunilda* would lose her magic charm. The mysterious realm in which she lives now would be gone, and the underwater creatures that form a kind of living cloak on her skeleton would die. Paddling out to McGarvey's Shoal, with views of Schreiber Channel, Mount Gwynne and the Slate Islands on either side, knowing the *Gunilda* was there in the waters beneath us, was a more vivid experience of history than seeing her weathered hull pulled up on land.

As we rounded the end of Nicol Island, the sun slipped through the crack of open sky between the clouds and horizon, illuminating the little village of Rossport to the north. Welcoming the sight of our last port of call before reaching Kama Bay, we put on some extra speed and hurried into the harbor. A large old boat, red, silver and green with the name *Yennek* painted on the stern, was tied up at a private dock. A woman on board was handing fishing rods and boxes to an elderly gentleman who wore a silver-painted pith helmet and an orange submersion jacket. He, in turn, was loading the equipment into a wheelbarrow. He helped the woman out, and then slowly and steadily pushed his load along the

One mid-November gale hurled spray and ice high enough to shatter the thick plate-glass windows surrounding the Battle Island Lighthouse light, 120 feet (36 m) above the lake.

Ray and Jos Kenney (right) and their friend, the late George Paradise, ninety-eight years old here and fondly known as the Judge, sit on the steps of Come and Rest cabin in the heart of the Slate Islands. Ray and Jos live in Rossport, where they spend their summers tending a garden, picking blueberries and fishing from their boat, the Yennek. They have shared with us a wealth of stories about life along the north shore.

dock. From the lane by the house, a curly-haired woman waved. Her yellow Labrador retriever took off like a shot, bounding straight toward the water, its tail wagging its whole body in glee.

"Hi, Schooner!" I heard the man say. By the conversation, we could tell it had been a successful day of fishing in the Slate Islands. Eager to find a place to camp before dark, I seized the opportunity of introducing ourselves.

Within moments, we were pushing the bows of our canoes into the long grass near shore and stepping out onto a shallow sandy bottom. Ray and Jos Kenney and their daughter, Colleen, insisted that we pitch our tent on the lawn and join them for the evening. Ed, their son, who had been working amid the potatoes and peas in the large vegetable garden, greeted us with equal warmth. It didn't take long before we realized that these four people looked at the world through bright and spirited eyes, a condition most surely fostered by a life on the shores of Lake Superior.

Sunset over the Rossport Islands.

The sight of a teepeelike shelter of driftwood is a reminder of a time long ago when people lived here year-round. They traveled in birchbark canoes and on snowshoes, hunting caribou and catching trout, whitefish and sturgeon. On the distant island, whose name means "thrown up by the wind," we discovered Pukaskwa pits on terraced beaches as large as football fields.

In the kitchen that evening, Ray and Jos cleaned their catch, a process perfected after more than sixty years of fishing together. We gathered around the kitchen table, Jos feeding us tea and toast while the stories flowed from Ray like a spring freshet. Topics ranged widely as the table disappeared under an array of photographs, framed prints and maps. About three o'clock in the morning, we drifted off to our tent. I couldn't sleep, so for another hour I scribbled in the logbook, describing Ray Kenney's crusade to save the Slate Island lake trout.

The Slate Islands produce a particular shallow water lake trout that almost looks like a speckled trout. Their diet of freshwater shrimp undoubtedly contributes to the fine taste and unique texture of the very red meat.

Apart from Ray's dedication to education, his lifetime passion had always been fishing. On weekends and all through the summer he would go fishing aboard the *Yennek*, out among the islands and the shoals. Ray knew where the fish were and people from all walks of life came to visit Rossport just to go out trolling with him. But in the 1950s, the catch began dropping off. "I've caught live fish with lamprey scars on them, but I've never seen any alive with the mark of a gill net." Ray's meaning was obvious. Knowing that the Slate Island trout spawning grounds would soon be empty due to the commercial catch, Ray circulated a petition to all the north shore businesses. He wrote hundreds of letters. In the end, the Slate Islands and the waters a mile out from shore received protected status. Now, forty years later, when there are very few naturally spawning lake trout left in Lake Superior, Ray and Jos are still able to troll through the Slates knowing the trout are swimming below. If it hadn't been for Ray's work several decades ago, the Slate Island trout would probably have gone the way of the Whitefish Bay whitefish.

Two nights and one day later, we slipped away from Rossport at daybreak. A square patch where the tent had been and our footprints through the frosty grass were all that remained of our stay. By the time the Kenneys awakened, those too would have evaporated with the sun. Turning west, we felt a light breeze brushing by, tickling the flat blue waters that stretched up Nipigon Bay. Not for the first time on the journey, I thought of wildebeests, antelopes and tiger converging on a watering hole on the other side of the world, predator and prey roles set aside in their quest for a much more vital part of living: water. I thought of all the people in the world waking up this morning, picking up their pails and walking to a well for water. And of the faucets in millions of homes turned on without a thought for the source of the substance pouring out. And here we were floating on it, a sea of fresh water so vast it had taken two and a half months to canoe around its shores.

On the final afternoon of our journey, we could see our destination, Kama Point,
from this place where the Jackpine River carves a serpentine path to Lake Superior.

Spruce and poplar form bands of dark green and gold along the red rock Kama Hills.

Sea kayaking on Kama Bay, the northernmost part of Lake Superior.

By mid-morning we were long past the Powder Islands and skirting Gravel Bay, with Simpson Island to the south. With a steady tailwind, we rode the rhythmic swell mile after mile, reflecting on our journey. Our crisp, clean maps of three months ago were scribbled and scratched with notes. The pictograph walls, beautiful campsites, historical references, names of people we had met along the way, nesting sites, questions to get answered, harrowing events on the journey, and dozens of places marked "must explore" and "must return."

We were already planning trips in other seasons on Lake Superior. Autumn hiking on Isle Royale and the Pukaskwa coast. Back-country skiing in Superior's old mountain ranges. Whitewater canoeing down the Dog, Sand, Goulais, White and Pukaskwa Rivers. A million pictures came to mind of now familiar places magically transformed by seasonal color — autumn's red, orange and gold, then winter's white, blue and purple, and spring's spectrum of greens. In the season of the winter moon, we imagined ourselves skiing where we now paddled, exploring icicle caves and frozen waterfalls, and listening to the orchestra of grinding and tinkling ice pans. Our ski and snowshoe tracks would cross the trails made by mice, rabbits, grouse, ravens, red fox, timber wolves and moose.

Opposite the high profile of hills on St. Ignace Island, we slipped around first one sand spit, and then another and another, until at last we could see Kama Point. And there, like an exclamation mark was Lillian Wolter, standing on the stony strand, waving excitedly — a scene reminiscent of our first roadside meeting several years back. Together Gary and I waved our paddles over our heads. The sight and feel of coming full circle, the end and the beginning merging as one, left me wondering for a moment if maybe I had just dreamed it all.

Circling the lake in canoes propelled by paddles, we had met Lake Superior on her terms, in the same way as those earlier inhabitants who left paintings, Pukaskwa pits, copper tools and stone weapons. In touching the water, the rocks and the great big sky, we left forever a part of ourselves to rest with all the spirits that have gone before us and all those that will come after. The wind on my face is their breath, my own heart beats in rhythm with the timeless song that binds us all. Within old cedars, dark forests, flowing rivers, polished pebble beaches and pure restless waves, mysterious life pulses on.

On a night in the Slate Islands, quiet contemplation around the campfire leads to thoughts of the islands' origins as a meteorite millions of years ago.

ACKNOWLEDGMENTS

Joanie and Gary would like to gratefully acknowledge the following companies and individuals for their support.

A number of dedicated people have been on the paper trail helping us to achieve our dream of printing this photographic book on totally chlorine free (TCF) paper. Laura Rose Day and Laura Hickey of the National Wildlife Federation and Archie Beaton of the Chlorine Free Products Association were especially instrumental in putting us in touch with SCHEUFELEN NORTH AMERICA, INC., the company that has provided paper for this book. The first print run of 10,000 copies required 24,000 pounds (10,800 kg) of paper. That's a lot of paper. Up until recently, bright white paper was achieved primarily through a bleaching process involving chlorine. Many toxic substances including dioxins enter our rivers and lakes from this common pulp and paper process. Swedish pulp mills, at the forefront of alternatives have developed closed-loop systems that employ oxygen and hydrogen-peroxide bleaching instead. Lake Superior is the best international symbol for clean, fresh water yet it is still affected by pollution from pulp and paper mills located along its shores.

We can all be more responsible consumers of paper, a product that touches our lives everyday. It is our hope that this book acts as an example of the alternatives available. The foresight and commitment of our Canadian publisher Boston Mills Press/Stoddart Publishing in choosing this paper serves as a model to other book publishers, printers, businesses, educational and government institutions. Such paper choices will create market demand and in turn inspire others in the pulp and paper industry to retrofit their mills with this improved technology. And every living thing benefits when we keep our fresh water clean.

John Denison, publisher of BOSTON MILLS PRESS, for his ability to interpret our vision for the book and for his unwavering faith, support and enthusiasm for holding this vision intact. Thanks also to Gill Stead, our intrepid book designer and Noel Hudson, Kathy Fraser and Stephanie Judy, the editors whose combined skills have worked their magic with our words and photographs to create this book. Besides that they are fun people to work with.

Richard Gulland at BLACKWATER DESIGNS in Foymount, who has outfitted us with SIERRA DESIGNS tents, sleeping bags, and the finest of fleece and Gortex outerwear to use on all our journeys. Thank you for keeping us warm and dry.

CONTAX – KYOCERA INC., for providing an RTS III camera and Zeiss lenses for this book and ongoing photographic projects. It goes without saying that our photographic equipment is of great importance to us. We really appreciate equipment that functions consistently under all conditions, even wet and cold! (All the photographs in this book were shot on Kodachrome 64 or Lumiere 100X slide film.)

Brian Henry and the crew at CURRENT DESIGNS, for providing the superbly constructed and designed sea kayaks; the Solstice ST and the Expedition models that enable us to extend our paddling season on Superior when weather conditions become more extreme. They also make it possible for us to explore some of the island groups a long distance from shore.

For twelve years we have been hiking over the hills and portages in NIKE footwear thanks to the company's ongoing support.

Brian Dorfman of the GREY OWL PADDLE CO., who has provided the fine wood canoe and kayak paddles for all our journeys over the years. A paddle is our connection between our canoe or kayak and the water; it gives us control over our destiny. Whether we are riding the long swells of Lake Superior en route to some distant island, or descending a twisting whitewater river, we put a lot of faith in the strength of those carefully handcrafted paddles.

Kay Henry and Rob Center of MAD RIVER CANOE, for providing us with the superb canoes we used to explore the Lake Superior watershed. For the eighty-day circumnavigation of Lake Superior we paddled Mad River Monarchs, 17'4" sea canoes that are partially decked. We could pack and portage them like canoes yet control our direction with a foot-operated rudder as in a sea kayak. This was an excellent feature for the solo canoeist-photographer! That we could lower the seats to the floor for more stability in wavey conditions was another welcome feature. The Monarch is our favorite long-distance solo canoe. On all the river trips, we paddled Mad River's ME and Flashback solo whitewater models. On other journeys with friends along the Lake Superior shore, we paddled a tandem Revelation, another excellent bigwater canoe. Every one of our friends who has canoe tripped on Superior with us in a Revelation now own one of their own. We would also like to thank Wayne Davenport and Gary Barton of ROCKWOOD OUTFITTERS–BLUEWATER CANOES, for their continuing support of our endeavors and for underwriting the import of Mad River canoes into Canada.

MEPHISTO, for providing financial support that greatly assisted us in undertaking journeys and obtaining photographs in all seasons in the Lake Superior watershed.

Alex Tilley of TILLEY ENDURABLES, who has not only provided continuing assistance for our endeavors as well as Tilley hats and clothing, but who is a kindred spirit when it comes to adventuring. Alex has pursued his own dreams and, along the way he has helped many others to achieve theirs.

Peter Spring of APACO IMAGING LABS produces the highest quality photographic prints from our photographs. It has been a dream of ours to produce a photographic exhibition of Lake Superior to accompany this book. Peter has shared our vision for this project and continues to produce our limited edition prints (see below).

LIMITED EDITION PHOTOGRAPHIC PRINTS from this book are available through the authors; Joanie and Gary McGuffin R.R.1 Goulais River, Ontario, Canada P0S 1E0 705-649-0671 by fax or telephone.

THE LAKE SUPERIOR SOUNDTRACK, entitled "Superior, Journeys On An Inland Sea," composed by Chris Mills is available on CD or tape from Boston Mills Press @ 1-800-565-3111. This musical interpretation of Superior combined with the lake's own songs was developed through experiences we have shared with Chris, Sally Ludwig, Ruth Fletcher and Ward Conway on Lake Superior. Thanks to Peter Maqua, for without Creation Cycle, we would never have met Chris.

ACKNOWLEDGMENTS

continued

For us, journeys are indeed a metaphor of life and at each twist and turn of the shoreline, the story changes course sometimes leading to unexpected and unexplained places. Journeying has not only taught us to adapt to ever-changing conditions; it has also opened up new worlds to us.

Superior, Journeys On An Inland Sea is a story about a physical endeavor, but beneath the surface, undercurrents flow with the emotional, intellectual and spiritual ties we have made with the land, the water, its life and, of course, the people we have met along the way. Thank you, all.

THE JOURNEY SOUTH
Lillian Wolter
Henry Schnellhardt
Lorne Saxberg
Heather Hagarthy
Peter Boyle
Pam Epps
Dick and Mary Gosling
David and Barb Olafson
Virginia Quick
Herb Wills
  and Sonja Helland
Vern and Terry McLaughlin
Jack Pichotta

THE JOURNEY EAST
Jeff and Mary, Josh, Matt
  and Kaitlin Gookins
Bob Brander
Tom Doolittle
Kayci Cook
Theresa Schenck
Henry and Lempi Heikkinen
Dorothy Heikkila
Judith Archibald
  and David Kenny
John and Evelyn Maki
Fred and Helen Waisanen
Bob and Chris Katzenitein

Hubert Mather
David Mataczynski
Frank Farwell
Fred and June Rydholm
Bill and Patty Mutch
Bill and Veryle Albrecht
Bud Velin
Raymond Romanski

THE JOURNEY NORTH
Betty Russell
Gayle Davey
Ruth Fletcher
  and Ward Conway
Lee Fletcher
John Mills
Ralph Mills
Sandy and Gary Sittler
Stephanie and Richard
  Raeburn-Gibson
Ann and Gordon Wyllie
Keith Quevillon

THE JOURNEY WEST
Dave Waddell
John Hieftje
Pukaskwa National Park staff
Vivian and Tim Alexander
Jos and Ray Kenney
Ed Kenney
Colleen Kenney
Judge George M. Paradise
Bert Saasto

Wayland Drew and Bruce Litteljohn, the authors of *Superior, The Haunted Shore*, who gave us their enthusiastic blessing to tell our story of the great lake. Thank you to Wayland for his writing, which continues to be a source of inspiration.

Lloyd and Ollie Moore, friends and pilots who safely and skilfully flew us along the entire north shore from Gargantua to Isle Royale so that we might obtain aerial photographs.

Loreen and Mervin McGuffin and Jennifer and John Wood, who are our best friends, a constant source of inspiration, and wonderful parents!

To all our friends here at Harmony Beach and Goulais River, our travels may take us far away at times, but your kindness, enthusiasm and neighborliness have ensured that our roots are firmly anchored in the Algoma Highlands on the shores of Lake Superior. For the first time in our lives together, we call a place home! Your influence in completing this project has been far greater than you probably realize.
Becky Adams and Mark Edwards
Vicki Anderson
Mary and Joe Calleri
Nino and Irma De Pauli
Andy Glibota and Madeline Wray

Robin MacIntyre and Enn Poldmaa
Bob Moore, John Ferguson and the White Pines highschool students
Mike and Carolyn O'Connor
Loretta and Dan Sweezey
Vaughan and Paula Ungar
Dianne Wadden
Jocelyn Watt

I would like to thank my mother, Jennifer Wood, and sister, Vivian Wood-Alexander, who read and reread this manuscript. And Robin MacIntyre, who also read the manuscript and provided many helpful comments and suggestions.

We really appreciated the fascinating insights into the lives of Superior's earliest human inhabitants given to us by Bill Ross, archeologist at the Ministry of Culture and Communications in Thunder Bay, and Mark Belanger on field trips to flint-knapping sites. Thanks to Mohiuddin Munawar at the Canada Centre for Inland Waters in Burlington, who provided us with much helpful information through his research on the liminology of Lake Superior.

Thanks to Gerry Bennett, a geologist at Northern Development and Mines, for reviewing the section on geology and providing helpful suggestions. And to Mr. R.E. Childerhose, Supervisor Aids

Operations and Maintenance, Transport Canada, for answering my questions on Lake Superior lighthouses. David Leddy at Michigan Technological University provided answers to our queries about the Keweenaw Peninsula's stamp sand beaches.

Thanks to the Sigurd Olson Environmental Institute for providing time, space, assistance and research materials. Lee Fletcher was most helpful in reviewing the story about Imogene Bay. And to Dan Pine, for his special words and wisdom, which reminded us to listen to our hearts.

And there are others, some friends, some professionals and some fellow travellers, who we would very much like to acknowledge with thanks for the varied ways in which they have also participated in this project.
Tom Bishop
Norm Bourgeois
Betty Brill
Gayle Coyer
Vicki Dorfman
Bill Gillin
Andrew Haill
John Haines
Bob Hansen
Grant Herman
Karlyn Holman

Bruce Hyer
Martin and Doris Ingles
Bill and Keefer Irwin
Bill Jerome
Sally Kessler
Todd Kessler
Kelly Kirchner
Tom Klein
Ruth Lull
Mary Ellen and Wayne
  MacCallum
John McHale
Chris Mills and Sally Ludwig
Vicki Nikkila
Ted and Gwen Nyman
Ruth and Gil O'Gawa
Mark Peterson
Mark Van Putten
Michael and Melanie Robinson
Birdie and Merce Romanec
Bill Rosenberg
Marilyn Smith
Mike Steele and Erin (Topper) Ryan
Pete and Kris Stinnissen
Jack Stokes
Cathy Sullivan
Greg Sweval
Pam Troxell
Hugh and Tammy Trueman
Richard Underdown
Beverley Viljakanin
Joe Weum
Mary Whitmore
  and Doug Dow